fierce & fabulous

The Feminine Force of Success

NKANDU BELTZ

Disclaimer

All the information, techniques, skills and concepts contained within this publication are of the nature of general comment only and are not in any way recommended as individual advice. The intent is to offer a variety of information to provide a wider range of choices now and in the future, recognising that we all have widely diverse circumstances and viewpoints.

Should any reader choose to make use of the information contained herein, this is their decision and the author and publishers do not assume any responsibilities whatsoever under any condition or circumstances. It is recommended that the reader obtain their own independent advice.

First Edition 2015

Copyright © 2015 by Nkandu Beltz

All rights reserved. No part of this publication may be reproduced, stored in a retrieval system, or transmitted in any form or by any means, electronic, mechanical, photocopying, recording or otherwise, without the prior written permission from the author.

National Library of Australia Cataloguing-in-Publication entry

Creator: Beltz, Nkandu, author.

Title: Fierce and fabulous : feminine force of success / Nkandu Beltz.

ISBN: 9780994184733 (paperback)

Subjects:
Inspiration – Anecdotes.
Success – Anecdotes.
Self-actualization (Psychology) in women.

Dewey Number: 158.1

Published by Author Express
www.AuthorExpress.com
publish@authorexpress.com

Dedication

All women who play
a bigger game, elevate
others, and measure
success in their own way.

Foreword

By Fiona Jones

I believe we all have our very own success story to share with the world. One that is as unique as our fingerprint. In order to do that, we often have lessons to learn or adversity we need to overcome. It's only then we can move on to our next chapter. Too many people get stuck, and in the process they sabotage their success story.

So often in our pursuit of success, we look to others and learn the rosy side of their story. We then paint a picture in our minds of a fantasy life, and when it doesn't quite turn out as we planned a host of maladies can occur. But in reality, life isn't always rosy. It's a constant balance of pleasure and pain. In this book Nkandu, and the women she has chosen to feature, courageously share their up-close and personal stories to reveal all facets of the story: the good, the bad, and the ugly.

Through the written word, these women are able to share their message, make a difference, and leave a legacy. A legacy doesn't need to be physical. It can be a property estate, a foundation, a charity, or even a book. It may be a song, a poem, or something you say that touches someone and changes their life. Legacies come in many forms, and often those who leave them may never know the people they affect. This in turn may cause a ripple effect of hope and inspiration.

The women in the book are driven by their personal passion to be fierce and fabulous, and they are now choosing to live in love, not fear. I'm absolutely passionate about books, as I believe they change lives. They've certainly changed mine. Think of all the people you've heard say, "I once read somewhere..." or "that book changed my life." It might have been one paragraph or one sentence that has never been forgotten. Sharing inspiring success stories was the entire inspiration for me to create *The Millionaire Books*.

Nkandu is a living example of someone who is making the change she wants to see in the world, and this book is another vehicle through which she is making that change happen. Wherever you are in your life right now, there is a reason you now hold the gift of this book in your hands. There are no accidents.

My hope is that by reading this book, you find that spark of light. Even if it's just a few words within the pages that inspire you to have the courage to choose LOVE over FEAR and to *Be Your Own Success Story*™.

Fiona Jones

Best-selling author and creator of *The Millionaire Books*
www.TheMillionaireSchool.com

FierceandFabulous.com.au

Acknowledgments

This is always the tricky part. I have so many people to thank, and I might miss a few.

I'm truly grateful to each and every person who is in my life. There are those who have challenged my vision and perception, as well as those who have supported me. I'm thankful to both. Nobody can grow without challenges.

I would like to pass my sincere gratitude to my mother, Ethel Mwale, for her unconditional love.

A tremendous thank you to my grandfather, PK Mwale. What a champion. All of his wisdom and love has stayed with me.

Thank you to my grandmother, Edina, for being fierce and fabulous.

A heartfelt thanks to all of the fabulous women featured in this book. It would not be possible without their inspirational stories. Therese, Tania, Fauza, Kelly, Sharron, Suzanne, Fur, Eva, Gaye, Jacinta, Chantal, Kia, Rebecca, Yeukai, and Philippa. Thank you so much for your time and patience.

I would also love to thank Dan from Creative Style House in Sydney for the book cover design.

Special thanks to my book mentors, Fiona Jones and Benjamin Harvey, from Author Express.

Thank you, Dr John Demartini, for believing in me and reminding me to play a bigger game.

My sincere thanks to Juraj Benak for all of the IT support and working on my websites and not giving up on me.

A big thank you to the Past Immediate Mayor of Yarra City, Jackie. Your support is highly appreciated.

To Heddie Goldburg, the Honorary Consul of Botswana, thank you very much for your support and encouragements.

To my Mentor James Gardner from UBS, thank you so much for the inspiration, pointing me in the right direction, and for all of the assistance and time you give of freely.

Thanks also to GirlPR for all of the media publicity and liaising with our sponsors.

I would like to thank our sponsors Pan Pacific Resorts, Sofitel Resort Melbourne.

To Mama Jan Owen, CEO, Foundation for Young Australians. I feel so much gratitude to have you in my life. You've taught me so many lessons and opened so many doors in my life. Thank you.

Thanks to The African Australian Community and the diplomatic community.

I would also like to pass my thanks to the loves of my life, Erik, Michelle, Claire, and Dr Beltz. You guys make this world a better place. I love you.

My thanks goes out to Caryn in the U.S.A. She made sure this book was written in English and not Bemba, my first Language.

Last but not least, I would like to give my sincere gratitude to my father Henry, he is a great man, and I'm such a lucky girl to have experienced his love, singing, and dance.

As a highly spiritual person, I would like to also thank the divine providence for making all of this possible.

Introduction

I was inspired to put this book together by my mother, Ethel. She is such a hard-working woman and beautiful on so many levels. Though she's had a hard life, I've never heard her complain.

This made me wonder what other women were going through and how they go about their day. How do they stay inspired? What does it mean to be a woman in business? I then went on a search to find women who are making a difference in their communities and tried to discover why they do what they do and how they do it. These women are superstars in their own right, but they don't go around announcing it to everyone, because they're so focussed on making a difference.

They have shared their strategies about how they overcame fear, how they survived physical and emotional violence, and most important, how to be fierce and fabulous every day. They are a true testament that any goal can be achieved if you set your mind to it.

I hope you find the following pages entertaining and thought provoking, and when you've finished the last page, you're left wanting more. I hope this book fills you with a sense of awe and gratitude. At times we all think we've been hit by the world's largest problem, only to find out that someone is not only surviving a much bigger problem, but they've found a way to deal with it and improve their lives because of it. My message is to be kinder to yourself and others. Take the time to look outward, beyond your own troubles, and reach out to someone. You could pull them from the edge.

You'll be happy to know you can connect with these women on social media, at various functions around the country, and their webinars. Please use this book as a manual to inspire you to go out and change the world.

Nkandu Beltz

Contents

Foreword
Acknowledgments
Introduction

Chapter 1:	Nkandu Beltz	1
Chapter 2:	Tania de Jong	13
Chapter 3:	Gaye O'Brien	21
Chapter 4:	Sharron Keating	33
Chapter 5:	Eva Sifis	47
Chapter 6:	Jacinta Petrie	65
Chapter 7:	Kia Dowell and Chantal Harris	87
Chapter 8:	Philippa Ross	111
Chapter 9:	Suzanne Waldron	125
Chapter 10:	Fauza Beltz	137
Chapter 11:	Fur Wale	145
Chapter 12:	Kelly Fletcher	165
Chapter 13:	Therese Howell	183
Chapter 14:	Rebecca McIntyre	205
Chapter 15:	Yeukai Ota	211
Conclusion		217
Resources		218
About The Author		219

"Some people succeed because they are destined, but most succeed because they are determined."

Henry Van Dyke

CHAPTER 1

Nkandu Beltz

Fierce & Fabulous ~ The Feminine Force of Success

Nkandu Beltz

I'm a philanthropist, speaker, and author. I've been recognised for my work in community groups across cultures and have developed successful initiatives such as the Youth Empowerment Program Australia (YEPA). Among my greatest accomplishments is interviewing important social leaders, including His Holiness the Dalai Lama.

For my own story, I asked myself the same questions I did of the other fierce and fabulous women whose stories make up this book. What path has led me to where I am today? What makes me feel fierce and fabulous? Who were my mentors? What have I learned along the way? In answering these questions, I hope I'm able to convey that any woman, from any walk of life, can be fierce and fabulous. That in fact you already are. You just have to tap into it.

I was born in a Katete, in the Eastern part of Zambia. It lies at the feet of the Mpangwe and Kangarema Hills, close to the Katete River. It's a small town, full of good people. The scenery there is beautiful, with its wildlife and the largest bird sanctuary in the country along the Luangwa Valley.

My parents encouraged me to put a hundred percent into everything I did. My mother was a home economics teacher, and my father was a manager at the Credit Union Saving Association of Zambia. Though not academically the best student in class, I took up a leadership role. I was actively involved in the drama club, and I excelled in acting and poetry. My major life-changing event was moving to Botswana from Zambia. I was a teenager, and I could see how the country was going down at a fast rate.

The political climate had changed drastically in Zambia, with the rich getting richer, and the poor getting poorer. There was no middle class anymore. My father lost his job. World Bank had pulled out of the country. Most of the workers had to leave, and my father was one of the last people to go. This meant we had to rely on my mother's income, but as a civil servant, she was not making enough money to sustain the family. We saw bread disappear from the table. Margarine became a luxury, and by that time we had to walk to school. I saw how my parents wanted to provide for the family. They sold the furniture, and soon we

CHAPTER 1: Nkandu Beltz

had to buy food from open markets instead of supermarkets.

My mum had to make a plan. She travelled to Botswana and got a job. The rest of the family went there, while my younger sister, Monique, and I remained in Zambia. We stayed with my Uncle Joseph and Aunty Jackie, and their little boy Josh for a few months to finish our exam year of junior high school. Uncle Joseph worked as an electrician with the Zambia Electric Service Corporation, the largest electricity company in the country. Aunty Jackie was a business lady. All I knew was that she was always busy. We lived in a two-story house in the posh suburbs, which meant my aunty and uncle were living a great life.

My sister and I spent most of our time at school. We would leave home at seven in the morning and come back at five pm, just in time for dinner, homework, and bed. We did miss our parents, and we spoke to them on the phone every other day. My young siblings would tell me about Botswana. The language, the people, and the food were different from Zambia, yet also similar in a lot of ways. For example, fat cakes. It's a simple mixture of flour, sugar, milk, and baking powder. In Zambia, we would eat the fat cakes with tea but in Botswana they would be accompanied by gravy and would be eaten during lunchtime.

After about three months, my dad came to collect us. We travelled to Botswana by bus and crossed the famous *Mosi-O-Tunia*, which means Smoke that Thunders. It's a place commonly known as the Victoria Falls.

There's something special about standing at the edge of the Victoria Falls. I guess it's being in the presence of magnificent beauty. I was captivated and in awe of what I saw. Even at that age, I understood that one had to take a moment in life to stop and appreciate what we can see and feel. Victoria Falls commands respect. You can't ignore its beauty. It's the same as the energy you feel in the presence of someone who is supremely confident. You can sense their greatness, and you're drawn to it. I felt like that when I interviewed the Dalai Lama.

The journey my mother took was not easy. Despite going through hard times and poverty, she still looked great with her high heels and good clothes. She did it with a smile and never complained. I feel I got these traits from her.

My sister, Monique, is two years younger than I am. We weren't just sisters, we were soul sisters. She went to a private school in the city, and I was at a public school. We both turned out okay.

Monique is now married and has two beautiful children. She's running a successful tourism company in Botswana. We're both strong women who are not afraid to speak our minds or follow our passion. I guess this trait might come from my grandmother, Edna, who has a strong character and a heart oozing with love.

I first realised the power of my femininity when I was eighteen. I was doing a part-time job at the Ngami-Times, a small local newspaper in Maun, Botswana. I had just finished high school, and I needed to work. I couldn't bear the thought of staying at home for three months waiting for the Cambridge results, so I asked my headmaster to write a reference to apply for a job as a freelance journalist. When I went for the interview, I was dressed as well as I could afford. If you want people to take you seriously, you need to look the part.

The daughter of the editor of the newspaper interviewed me, and she was obviously a no-nonsense type of person. She asked me why I thought I could have the job without any experience. I was nervous and shaking inside but told her I was good at it and could do the job. I was completely faking my self-confidence, but it worked. This taught me that as fierce and fabulous woman, we need to be able to make decisions quickly and with confidence.

My first job was to do court reporting and social events. I enjoyed my work. I walked with pride, and I took my job seriously. The lessons I learned from that interview have stayed with me throughout my life. I was given an opportunity, and I took it. This helped me to believe in myself, and of course it boosted my ego. At that stage, I already started actively seeking mentors, and the Director for the Media Institute of Southern Africa took me under his wing.

I was soon on the A-list in Maun. I interviewed the president of Botswana and went backstage at concerts with international musicians. I interviewed criminals who'd been accused of robbing banks, as well as everyday people. Every morning I woke up and got ready to do it all over again, because I knew this was what I wanted to do, and I was getting paid to do it. Even as a teenager, I knew I had to set up a firm foundation of a good work ethic and continuous education.

The lessons learnt in Botswana helped me get into events after arriving in Australia. In 2011, I presented the summary of the Commonwealth Youth Forum *Communiqué* that provides young Commonwealth citizens the opportunity to

CHAPTER 1: Nkandu Beltz

discuss issues and share their experiences. Delegates from all Commonwealth nations attend the event, and a final *communiqué* document is produced and presented to heads of governments.

From over a hundred youth from all Commonwealth countries, I was one of three representatives asked to present the *communiqué* to the Foreign Ministers meeting. Australia's then Foreign Minister, Kevin Rudd, was chairing. I was a little nervous but at the same time, excited. I executed the talk and kept reminding myself my reason for being there. I was representing 1.5 billion youth across the Commonwealth countries. It was a fierce moment for me to lend my voice to people who can't speak for themselves or don't have the opportunity to have their voices heard. It's an honour to use my talents and gifts to help improve people's lives.

I've always had big dreams, and this included having a family. Running my own business, being in a supportive and loving relationship, having a great circle of friends, and just making sure my seven areas of life are balanced. Those are: social, physical, career, financial, family, spiritual, and mental.

The people who have helped me to become fierce and fabulous would first of all be my grandfather. His grace and gratitude set an example for me. He's a down-to-earth man who can dine with kings, mix with common people, and remain humble. He's a hard-working man, and I love him dearly.

My mentor and film director, Owas Ray Mwape, is another. Mr Mwape always believed in me and encouraged me to dream big. He would push me to give my all when I was in his acting class and encourage me to use my voice. I remember one time during rehearsal he stopped me halfway through my lines and pointed out that my voice was weak. He told me I needed to improve the tone, as well as the projection, and remember to breathe. These lessons still stick with me today. I use them whenever I'm on stage or speak in meetings. We're powerful beings, and playing it small does not serve anyone.

My husband is my strongest supporter. I met Erik when I was twenty, and we got married eight months later. He has supported me every step of the way and cheered me on. When the going gets tough, and I want to throw in the towel, he reminds me why I started the project. He's so honest and tells me bluntly if I'm wasting my time on a project or if the idea is at all worthy of pursuing.

It's so important as women to have a good support system. I've been fortunate to find that in Erik. We sit at the table and brainstorm ideas. It's a family affair, and sometimes I invite my friends to give me feedback before we go to market. I believe in having a team. You can never succeed by yourself. We need to help each other and share our ideas.

I had a plan. I feel a major act of bravery was deciding to have three children before I turned thirty. When I was young, I would play house with my friends, and I would always be the mother. A mother who was wearing heels, a mother who would drop and pick up her kids from school. A mother who would follow her dreams.

I did manage to reach some goals. I've always had a clear plan as to what I wanted out of life. This doesn't mean everything has gone according to my plan. I've made choices and taken chances. That's life. Ten percent is just living, and the other ninety percent is how we react to the situations around us.

My three pregnancies were difficult. I spent a lot of time in hospital due to severe morning sickness and dehydration, but the minute the kids were born, all of that was forgotten. I fell in love with them. First Michelle, then Claire, and last, Erik Jr. I was still studying journalism, and it did slow me down, but I persevered and succeeded at my studies. During my years as a young mother with small children, I worked part-time at the radio station as a broadcaster, and I wrote for the local newspaper. I also read as much as I could in the evening. Parenting can be challenging, but then again, I had a team of friends to help me. Of course I would do the same for them. You get what you give. I now have three adorable darlings who are such an important part of my universe, and I cherish them with gratitude.

Another vision I had was to run my own business doing speaking engagements, writing, and producing TV programs. I managed to make it happen. I speak in schools and universities, as well as at clubs. I have been asked to MC corporate and private functions. My speaking is focussed on self-development and management. I encourage people to make the best of what they have. I'm also a mentor to many young people around the country. Topics range from cyber bullying to respectful relationships and women's rights.

CHAPTER 1: Nkandu Beltz

Since I was a child, I always wanted to travel the globe and live abroad. I was born in Zambia, lived in Botswana and The Netherlands, and now I'm an Australian Citizen. Future visions involve writing more books, hosting my own TV show/documentary, and building a business school in Zambia for girls.

My vision board has a few ticks of the people I've always wanted to meet. One of them was His Holiness the Dalai Lama. I interviewed him two years ago. Dr John Demartini was another. He is such a nice guy and a great teacher. Others on my list I have not had the pleasure to meet yet are Oprah Winfrey, Richard Branson, Hillary Clinton, and Desmond Tutu.

The Obamas inspire me, because they made their dreams into reality. These are people just like you and me. The only difference is they've taken action and have so much courage. But I can't compare myself to them. They're on chapter ten, and I'm on chapter one. I respect them for what they do, and I know I have it within me to accomplish great things.

But all of the awards, achievements, and success stories in the media are just part of the bigger picture. I feel we have a long way to go as a society. We still have people dying from preventable diseases, extreme poverty, and killings in the name of religion. Women's rights are still questioned, and a lot of women are still suppressed. We're seeing an increase in the movement of the modern feminist. This is not a fight for equal rights. It's a human rights issue. My greatest accomplishments would be to help people believe in themselves and take action.

I'm happy with my life so far. I'm an independent woman in all areas of life. That makes a big difference in my self-esteem. I always tell my friends that you can never dis-empower an empowered woman. I have the courage, I have the drive, and I know my rights and responsibilities, so it's hard for anyone to walk all over me. But I pick my fights, and sometimes I have to let go of smaller issues to focus on bigger and better ones. For example, some people still have a problem with me being a young, working mother. I don't let such things sink into my head, because everyone will have an opinion as to what I should be doing or wearing or eating. I know what I want, and I know how to get it. I love my family, and I have a big plan to help serve humanity. We're in this together.

When I look in the mirror, I see a beautiful girl with big dreams who's on her way to achieving them. But I also see a confident woman who is wildly successful on her own terms. A fierce and fabulous young woman. My hope and dream is to continue working with young people by creating meaningful projects to help our communities thrive. Everything I do has to benefit others. I ask myself each morning, "How can I be of great service to those around me?"

There is a difference between servitude and being a servant. The service I offer comes from my heart. It's genuine, and I enjoy giving. I feel like if I died today, I would tell God that I did my best for Him and mankind. Every morning, I go through everything I'm grateful for in my life, and I mean *everything*, including the clean air I breathe, the warm shower I take, the food on the table, and the gift of life and health.

However small they may seem, your decisions have an impact on you and the quality of your relationships with others. Whatever you do or say can either make someone happy or break them down. Your actions speak the loudest. No act of kindness is ever wasted. One thing I've learnt through this journey of who I am and who I want to be is that sometimes your best is not good enough. You will find people who want to take and not give back. Do not let this deter you from your path. Stay true to yourself, and follow your gut feeling.

My childhood helped me build a solid foundation and create myself into a woman who believes in herself. I had the privilege of learning and knowing about my roots. What my people before me did, and the care they gave. I can never be broken, only bent. Change starts inside of me and goes out to the world. I started realizing I could make a difference. When I spoke, people listened and acted. They wanted to help. I always believed I was born to make a difference.

The realisation of who I am as a person did not happen overnight, and sometimes I still ask myself "Who am I?" But one thing I know is that I'm a significant human being who is part of an awesome team called the human race. I know for sure that if you surround yourself with people you admire, who add value to your life, who are interested in your development as a person, you will move to higher ground. Never settle for mediocrity.

CHAPTER 1: Nkandu Beltz

AscendSmart Institute

About us

AscendSmart Institute is a private company consisting of a small group of dedicated individuals committed to inspiring and empowering individuals and organization to be the best they can be. We believe you can't be an effective change maker if you're not inspired from within. We work with a team of local professionals and partners to make sure your child gets the best out of this program

About the Director

Our founder, Nkandu Beltz, is passionate about youth development. She has built the curriculum based on her accumulated fifteen years of experience in the not-for profit sector and other various organizations. She is an author and one of Australia's leading social change makers.

Courses:

High Tea with a Purpose for Teens

Young girls struggle to find their place in society while developing their self worth and self esteem. At the pre-teen age, their peers easily influence them.

We've designed a program specifically for girls from ten to fourteen years of age. Our main focus is on building their self worth and helping them step up and be their authentic self.

The best gift you can give a child is to help them build a strong foundation and learn the skills to be an independent individual in a world where the media has determined what a girl should look like. We celebrate individuality and understand each person is unique, while also defining what binds all of us together.

High Tea with a purpose for Primary and Secondary Schools

Some of the topic your children will learn:
- Body image/ Being your authentic self
- Posture and presence
- Getting rid of limiting beliefs (you can do it)
- Self worth and respect
- Friends
- Attitude
- Nutrition
- Skincare and hair tips

We know that an individual who manages to present herself with confidence and poise in everyday life will be seen by herself and others as a person who matters.

Fierce and Fabulous: The Feminine Force of Success

This high tea is an opportunity for businesswomen to have a deeper conversation about what it means to be a woman in business. To get to the bottom of the real issues nobody is talking about:
- Balancing life and work.
- How other women manage to have children and still be on top of their game.
- Creating a support network and what happens when the dark clouds visit. The shadow no one wants to acknowledge.

We are a vibrant community of women in business who are passionate about sharing the resources, networks, and business intelligence with you.

Our channels include an online community and face-to-face events programs.

CHAPTER 1: Nkandu Beltz

STEMSEL: Teaching young people to code.

STEMSEL stands for Science Technology Engineering Maths Social Enterprise Learning.

ezSystem is a graphical software interface that allows you to quickly and easily program micro-controllers. The software was originally designed for engineers by our technology partner, eLabtronics, but was found to be so easy to use, a child could program it. As a result, eLabtronics has released the simplified version for STEMSEL, and this forms the backbone of our teaching program. ezSystem offers a graphic of the board to simplify port selection. Then it sends information to its sub-program, CoreChart, which offers a flowchart-based programming language that is quick and easy to understand.

Media Training for Authors and Small Businesses

Nkandu Beltz Media Consultancy specializes in training clients to become effective media spokespeople for their projects and how to posit them on a platform to help get their message across.

The media is a powerful force in today's society, because of their ability to influence opinions and shape events. Everyone needs to be able to communicate effectively.

The Nkandu Beltz Media Consultancy Course will help you develop the skills to:
- be an effective spokesperson
- define your media message
- harness the power of the media by understanding their needs

Other Services:
- Book Writing: Stories that Inspire
- Public Speaking
- Master of Ceremony
- Keynote Speaker
- Life Coaching One on One

"Personal growth happens just outside your comfort zone."

Gaye O'Brien

CHAPTER 2

Tania de Jong AM

CHAPTER TWO

Tania de Jong AM

Tania is a leading Australian soprano, inspirational speaker, social entrepreneur, creative innovation catalyst, and spiritual journeywoman. She founded Creativity Australia, Creative Universe, MTA Entertainment & Events and The Song Room. She also works with disadvantaged communities through Creativity Australia's 'With One Voice' choir social inclusion programs. Tania presents keynote speeches and leadership programs. She performs internationally as a soloist and with her group Pot-Pourri, with whom she's released seven CDs. She is Founder and Executive Producer of Creative Innovation Global, and Tania's TED Talk How Singing Together Changes the Brain, has sparked international interest. In 2015 Tania released her solo CD Heaven on Earth.

Tania's awards include Ernst and Young Australian Social Entrepreneur of the Year, Outstanding Individual Contribution to Australian Culture, Churchill Fellowship, and the Accessibility Award in The Melbourne Awards. She was inducted into the AGSE Entrepreneurs Hall of Fame at Swinburne University and named Brainlink Woman of Achievement. She was appointed a Member of the Order of Australia in June 2008 for service to the Arts as a performer and entrepreneur, as well as through the establishment and development of music and arts enrichment programs for schools and communities.

Tania's mission is to change the world, one voice at a time.

When I interviewed Tania, my goal was to find out how it all started, why she chose her life path, and the impact she feels she's made.

How do you feel about singing as a form of expression?

A lot of Australian children and adults are silenced when they try to sing, which is in stark contrast to countries such as Africa or the South Pacific nations like Vanuatu or Fiji, where everyone sings with their families in harmony in church

CHAPTER 2: Tania de Jong

and in the community. They sing, celebrate and stick together. It's only in this western culture we have this judgment that people can or can't sing. In fact, we were born to sing. As human beings, our voice is part of our DNA. Tribes who sing and dance together survive!

When we aren't able to express ourselves in this way, it's not healthy. I encourage everyone to find their voice, and I don't just mean their singing voice. Don't allow yourself to be silenced in any way. Through the neuroscience of singing, we help people change their neural pathways. Singing changes people's brains and helps them to get into a more positive, creative headspace. Singing makes you smarter, healthier, happier and more creative.

What is Creative Innovation Global?

As Founder and Executive Producer of Creative Innovation Global, I curate and produce the acclaimed Ci2010 toCi2015 conferences. Ci2013 was named Corporate Event of the Year in the Global Eventex Awards and Ci2015 was named in The Anthill SMART 100. It's also a finalist in The Australian Event Awards. Creative Innovation Global is now regarded as the leading future-shaping innovation conference in Australasia, attracting delegates and speakers from around Australia and internationally. Ci events are for leaders and emerging talent across all sectors and feature an Innovation Leaders Scholarships program. Ten scholarships are awarded annually to emerging entrepreneurs and innovators from around Australia.

I support entrepreneurs, and that's why we have innovation scholarships at the conference. Many of the people who've won those scholarships have gone on to incredible achievements. I believe in supporting people who aren't afraid to take risks. The conference is for those who want to transform people's thinking.

Technology is disrupting business as we know it. We need to understand and embrace this new world. These conferences help people manage disruption and understand what the acceleration in technology and changes in our world mean.

What are some of the challenges when you set up a charity like Creativity Australia?

Creativity Australia is building a happier, healthier, more inclusive nation. We bridge the gap between people experiencing disadvantage and those more fortunate, through the neuro-scientific benefits of community singing. We build supportive networks that help people connect to brighter futures.

Our key challenge is to have to constantly raise funds to ensure we have the resources to fulfil our mission. Another major challenge is finding the talented people who are prepared to work for a charity for less money than they would earn in the corporate sector. Many people are searching for meaning and purpose in their lives and work. That helps in attracting talent into the not-for-profit sector.

In order to ensure Creativity Australia becomes sustainable, we've launched a major fundraising campaign called *Sing for Good*. We launched on the first of August in 2015. Groups of two or more from any family, club, school, community, or workplace, sing a song of their choice. Then they video it, put it on YouTube, and get their friends and networks to vote for them, as well as donate to support those in need. Funds raised support disadvantaged people who suffer from depression, disabilities, unemployment, migrants, older people and those who are isolated. We have lots of different categories like Best Female Sing, Best Blokes, Hospitals, Schools, Foreign Language and Best Family Sing. Then on November 8. 2015, we'll have a huge concert called *With One BIG Voice* at the Melbourne Town Hall, where we'll announce the winners and have a community big sing featuring fourteen of our *With One Voice* choirs from three States.

What are some of your life-changing events?

I've had many life-changing events. Being told a few times not to bother having singing lessons was life-changing, because I had to find the strength to keep going on the path I knew was right for me.

When my relationship of twenty years broke up, that was life-changing, especially because it was with my partner with whom I've sung for nearly thirty years in our group, Pot-Pourri. We travelled the world together singing and released seven CDs.

I think setting up both of my charities was life-changing. It's always much harder to set up anything from scratch and change the status quo.

I discussed this in my TED talk. I sing with a girl in our *With One Voice Melbourne* choir who has Cerebral Palsy. She's changed my life for sure. She always tells me

CHAPTER 2: Tania de Jong

the program is the highlight of her week. I just think to myself, *How lucky am I?* It gives you a sense of gratitude. I could be her, and she could be me. It's just the luck of the draw. It's changed my whole life, because it's made me realise just how lucky I am. When I'm having a grumpy day, I see this girl or get an email from people whose lives we're changing, or complete strangers come up to give me a hug, and it puts everything in perspective. I'm so grateful for what I have.

Would you like to share some of your favourite quotes?

One is by Rabbi Hillel. "If I am not for myself, who will be for me? And if I'm only for myself, what am I? And if not now, when?" The next one is Mark Twain. My CD, *Heaven on Earth*, is named after this quote:

> "Sing like no one is listening,
> love like you've never been hurt,
> dance like nobody is watching,
> and live like it's Heaven on Earth."

Then there's another one I really like by Churchill. "We make a living by what we get, but we make a life by what we give."

What are some of your greatest accomplishments, and how do you feel people limit themselves?

I think being able to change the status-quo and help people find their true creative voice is one of my greatest accomplishments. I love to join the dots between diverse people and make things happen where nothing was happening before. When I look in the mirror, I see someone who will continue to change the world, and the only thing stopping her is her own self-belief…and a lack of time to do everything. When I'm performing there's a sense that I'm doing what I'm born to do. What I'm called to do. Not only when I sing, but when I speak as well.

I always tell people not to be afraid to fail and to consider it a learning experience. FAIL = First Attempt In Learning. We have a risk-averse culture in Australia, but we have to acknowledge that we're probably going to fail a number of times before we'll succeed. I've failed plenty of times in my life. You need to take risks, even when everyone is saying you won't succeed. I was told the charities and conferences would never work. If I'd listened to them, I wouldn't have done anything. Believe in yourself, build a supportive team and network, think outside the box, and partner with diverse people and organisations.

Don't just hang around with people like you. Have positive, human collisions with people who take you outside of your comfort zone. Diversity is the key to innovation and creative behaviour. Walk your talk. Actions speak louder than words, so don't be a *gonna* person. Don't say I'm *gonna* do this and I'm *gonna* do that. If you come up with an idea, do it with all your heart and soul. Don't be afraid to let your individual voice be heard.

CHAPTER 2: Tania de Jong

Creative Universe

At Creative Universe, we've identified that transformation happens through creativity, so we make the extraordinary possible by helping to create sustainable, aligned, and high-performance organisations. Our goal is to help develop creative leaders and build a culture of innovation.

We build capabilities in creative thinking and leadership, develop a culture of innovation and entrepreneurship, assist in understanding and managing disruption, foster diversity and community, and unleash the potential of individuals and teams.

We offer a range of innovative leadership programs, speakers, performers, conferences, and special events to inspire your most important asset: your people. Through engaging with our transformational programs, you will realise the performance and creative potential of your people and organisation.

Our channels for change include Creative Innovation Global, Inspiring Minds creative leadership, capability and team building programs, Tania de Jong AM and other inspirational keynote speakers, outstanding Australian group Pot-Pourri and MTA Entertainment and Events production company. We also support Creativity Australia's transformational *With One Voice* social inclusion programs.

Creative Universe is about what has never been…the art of possibility!

CHAPTER 3

Gaye O'Brien

"Passion is energy. Feel the power that comes from focusing on what excites you."

Oprah Winfrey

CHAPTER 3: Gaye O'Brien

CHAPTER THREE
Gaye O'Brien

Gaye O'Brien provides leadership workshops to corporations and small businesses around the world to help them navigate a pathway toward their goals, dreams, and aspirations, so they can show their magnificent selves to the world.

I first met Gaye at a leadership program, Expert Accelerator, run by Benjamin Harvey. I was fascinated by her work, and after hearing her story, I decided she was most definitely fierce and fabulous and would inspire women around the globe.

Tell me about your early life.

I was born and raised in a small western town in Central Queensland. It's the same place where Quentin Bryce, the former Governor-General of Australia, was also brought up. My parents were raised during the depression of the 1930s, so they were keen to provide a good living for the family. They worked hard and gave us all of the opportunities they didn't have.

I was born during prosperous times, but I do remember my father telling me stories about the depression and how he had to drink goat's milk and eat goat's meat, and they grew their own pumpkins. That's what they survived on, because they lived in the bush. There wasn't much water. They didn't grow many vegetables. It was pretty tough times for them.

What was some of the best advice your parents gave you?

My father always said I needed a profession or a trade, otherwise I would struggle. That always stuck in my mind. It made me want to make the most of my time on this planet. That's the burning drive for me. I want to make the most of every day, and I want to be the best I can be and help others do the same.

What was some of your early work experience?

I've had some adversities that have made me work even harder to achieve what I have. I worked in the education industry, which is not easy. That gave me the resilience to move forward and also help others realise they can have a better life for themselves. That's what's pushing me forward.

In 2006 after I got married, I was working in a managerial position for the government and got quite burnt out with my job.

How did you manage the stress?

I started meditating and explored other methods as well. I also wanted to develop better communication, so that whenever I was in a social situation, I would communicate more effectively and have a more meaningful experience with the people I was talking to.

I'd made other attempts in the past, so I knew what not to do. I changed my routine. For instance, instead of watching movies like I used to do for stress relief, I decided to include meditation. It was simply a matter of dropping what didn't work and taking on a behaviour that would get me better results. I'd always had this pattern of talking myself through things. Of being disciplined. I'd just keep telling myself I could do it, but I never punished myself. If I didn't accomplish everything I wanted, I told myself I could always do more the next day. All I did was find a technique. It's about consistency. It's about creating a space where you won't be disturbed and just doing it.

If necessary, you can reward yourself in some way to keep yourself on track, because you will see your life change for the better. I've seen amazing results. I have so much more patience and empathy, and I'm much calmer. It overflows into all of my relationships, but the best thing is that I'm so focussed. My mind doesn't wander anymore, and I don't have any of this chatter going on in my head and gnawing at me. Focus has been the biggest single advantage, and I think a lot of women would love that. Women quite often have so many things going on at once, so if we can find a way to focus, even if it's only for a few minutes, it can be invaluable. It relaxes you and makes you feel like you're achieving something. And it's enjoyable.

CHAPTER 3: Gaye O'Brien

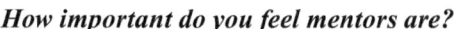

How important do you feel mentors are?

It's so important to talk to people who have walked the path you want to walk. We all grow up with a certain view of life based on our personal experiences. If you want to break out of your limited vision, you need to model yourself on someone who's done it. That's why a woman like Oprah is such a great role model. She started with nothing, yet she developed a pathway toward her goals without it being in her immediate environment.

I met my partner when I was only eighteen. I noticed he had lots of wonderful qualities, and I think he's always been a mentor. His parents have also been my mentors. In more recent years I've studied with a lot of the leading people in the personal development industry all around the world, and I have accumulated great mentors there as well.

Without resilience, it's easy to give up and sink down into that *poor me* mindset and think you don't deserve it or you can't do it or you're having a run of bad luck. I think a way to develop resilience is to have a routine, or what I prefer to call it, a ritual. Even if it's to go for a walk, to meditate, to eat well, or to think good thoughts. This ritual will give you focus, and then that focus will give you certainty about your life. Once you get certainty, you feel more confident to seek out mentors and develop skills. Then you'll achieve your goals. I'm a great believer in getting inspired by mentors. I study, watch a lot of videos, and read a lot of books. I'm always filling up my tank, even if it's being depleted by people around me. My writing really keeps me going. It keeps me focussed and inspired.

What did you have to give up to achieve your goals?

For me to achieve what I wanted, I eventually had to give up my job and the security of a regular income. Once you become an entrepreneur, and you're relying on the whim of the market to provide you with an income, it's a bit more risky than having a day job where the money flows in. It's a riskier path, but it's a more invigorating, fun, and interesting one.

My family members have their own businesses, so they know the ups and downs of it, but they still sometimes look at me and wonder what I'm doing. They say I could sit back and live a life of leisure. They think I should just spend time with the family. I think there's enough room for it all. We're living in such a changing world. We've got to keep our mind active to keep up with those changes, because otherwise we'll be left behind, and what sort of an example would that set for our children? I just tuned it out and stuck to my routine. Even when I had a regular job, I got up early and wrote. I've always had this focus, this vision. I did visualisations and kept on going.

Sometimes I did fall flat on my face, but I picked myself up and took the time to get some fresh inspiration.

Why do you think some people don't reach their goals?

A lot of people don't have a vision. They don't have a plan. They're depressed. They're anxious and worried about what they don't want. This is not living. We're only here for a short amount of time, so why not make the most of it? I do what I do, because I want to make a difference in the world. What I love is to inspire individuals and businesses to be the best they can be and help the planet. I do it through my webinars and seminars, as well as my articles, books, coaching programs, and speaking.

I have a passion for the possible. Quite often we're put down, but we can change our programming. I help people change the programming in their heads, so that they can be all they want to be. I studied early childhood education when I was eighteen. It made me realise how important the brain is and how we don't use it. People need to stretch their brains to do what they think is impossible. Our greatest learning comes just outside of our comfort zone.

How do you help people break out of this pattern?

I run a mastermind program for businesses. It's called The Business Accelerator Process, where people are encouraged to set a vision and develop a ritual, as well as set goals and review what they've done. I encourage them to be conscious about what they want, and then look at themselves and ask what they need to do. They're asked what mindset they need to have to follow their vision, and we set up steps towards achieving this vision. Businesses don't fail. People fail businesses, so I encourage business people to seek out all of the possibilities and help them set up a plan. Then we set up another plan and another plan, and another plan, so that they no longer see only one path to their success. Otherwise when something goes wrong, they could go into stress and adrenal

CHAPTER 3: Gaye O'Brien

mode and not know how to cope. This is why part of the program is helping them to master their emotions, so that they can manage stress.

My website is www.gayeobrien.com. I do coaching, Time Line Therapy, and hypnotherapy. My belief is that you have to clear out the stuff from the past to move forward and focus on the present. I also work with people who aren't in business, for instance those transitioning out of marriages or from one career to the next, or from a career to a business. I assist people who are struggling in their careers and do values alignment work. People want to see the relevance of where they are with the job they do.

People struggle with change. They're struggling with transitions, and they're struggling with their own heads. Our old brain and emotions still run the show. I assist people in using more of their new brain. Their thinking brain. It's this brain that enables you to focus and get the job done. It's about mind management and going where you want to go.

I lead an international women's spiritual group. We meet on Skype every fortnight and explore different ways of helping us find our purpose. There are different exercises we go through. I'm also in the process of developing an online program.

What is your vision for the future?

My bigger vision is that I can see people co-creating and collaborating a lot more, and by doing that they will conserve the planet's resources. The internet has allowed the most amazing opportunities for us to be able to work together. My goal is to help people around the world create the vision of themselves they want to be.

Everyone has the ability to understand they don't have to repeat the same pattern over and over and that life can be different for them. I'm developing a whole series of videos that will be part of the online program. It's all slowly coming together. I just want to give people the same opportunities I've had.

Do you have advice for women on how to reach their goals?

Women need to see the possibilities. To go for it and not give up. Stay the course and seek support. They need to recognise that if someone is putting them down or saying they shouldn't be doing something, it's a reflection on that person and not them.

These are the three ideas I'd like to share.

1. There is a greater expression inside you yearning to come out and help you reach your potential.
2. Embrace your personal power and move forward each day with the clear intention of doing good in the world.
3. Each of us is responsible for raising awareness, making a contribution, and inspiring those around us to play a bigger game.

Often we're surrounded by people who won't take responsibility for their own lives. But when you think about it, I guess it's always been that way, and there will always be a small percentage of the world that keeps the whole show going. I read a book where it talked about how there are ten people who keep the world vibrating at a high level, because so much of the population vibrates in a negative range. For instance, saints, martyrs, and spiritual leaders. I met a group of people recently. One of them was an Indian elder from one of the tribes. He flew to the Australian desert, because he intuitively knew that's where he needed to be in order to raise the vibrations. These people move around the world and keep the vibrations balanced.

The way we get to that place is by meditating and keeping balanced. Be conscious in every moment about how you're feeling. If you're not feeling right, think a better thought. You can always do something to move your vibration up to the next level. You don't need to get to a high level of elation or incredible love for everybody. Just take the next step, whatever that is. It might be getting up from in front of the TV and sweeping the floor. Whatever the next step is for you, stretch yourself a little bit so you feel better, because when your vibrations are higher, you attract better situations into your life. You need to use yourself as your best tool. If you decide to use the practice of developing rituals, you can do it anytime, anywhere. That calmness is great to be able to pass on to your children.

CHAPTER 3: Gaye O'Brien

New Life Solutions

New Life Solutions Mission Statement: Co-create meaningful experiences in a more enlightened world by motivating businesses and individuals to make their greatest contribution to the planet and to adopt a positive and open mindset towards everything they do.

New Life Solutions is passionate about helping people become all they can be. Gaye brings with her a wealth of experience from the business, education, media, and health sectors and currently hosts the radio show, "Passionate About Possibilities."

NLS acknowledges how busy life can be and is dedicated to enabling you to walk away with the necessary mindset, tools, systems, and support to create a rewarding lifestyle, business, or career you're proud to promote and talk about to your friends, family, clients, and the world.

NLS is a catalyst for transformational change in business. Gaye O'Brien coaches, speaks with, and provides leadership workshops to companies to enhance their performance by increasing their customer base, maximizing their profits, and systematizing their business to reduce time spent in the business. She's aware of the challenges businesses face and skilfully coaches corporations and small businesses around the world to navigate a pathway towards their goals, dreams, and aspirations, so they can show their magnificent selves to the world.

NLS offers a professional, tailored, unique, "5 Keys to Inner Success" process that is reasonably priced and includes personal coaching, live events, and on-line programs for individuals and organizations. People who have big dreams for the future are empowered to develop their highest potential by discovering their passions, values, and beliefs, discarding their limiting beliefs, and implementing stress reduction, time management, and goal-setting techniques to embrace peak performance in their lives, relationships, business, and health.

Clients who attend our coaching programs or workshops enjoy the small-group environment and are able to make long-term positive changes to their business or life as long as they remain committed to the process. The programs are also fully guaranteed.

The Birth of New Life Solutions

New Life Solutions was founded in 2008 after Gaye experienced stress due to her role as a Leading Teacher and Manager in the teaching and training profession. She recognized that there must be an easier way to be more productive in the workplace, communicate more effectively, develop better rapport, and manage conflict. Gaye found the techniques to be effective with managing emotions, elevating energy levels, and getting along better with others.

Gaye resigned from her successful career to establish her own business, as she felt it would give her greater flexibility in assisting others to make the necessary changes to improve their lives. Many mentors have assisted her to develop her eclectic approach.

CHAPTER 3: Gaye O'Brien

Some testimonials:

Today I found inspiring. I am excited about the changes I will achieve in order to improve and fulfil my life's desires.

~Michelle Kraatz

I have gained skills in realizing what I want and how to get it

~Kayleen Clark

Gaye O'Brien is a fully qualified and certified Life, Business and Executive Coach, NLP Trainer, Time Line Therapist, Hypnotherapist, and international best-selling author of *NLP Essentials for Teachers*.

"Nothing will work unless you do."

Maya Angelou

CHAPTER 4

Sharron Keating

Chapter Four

Sharron Keating

Sharron is the owner of Epicure Coaching, a service that helps businesses create dynamic teams. She works with business owners who've lost focus and direction, whether it's their business, their team, or life itself. She helps them overcome these problems quickly, so they can move forward and gain control of their business.

Both Sharron and her partner, Mat, have two kids and run a café, so I wanted to find out how they were able to balance all of their responsibilities. Sharron and I had our first interview in her well-maintained home where you'd never guess two young boys ran around most of the day, but it goes to show that when you put systems in place, life is more easily managed.

Tell me about your early life.

I was born in Adelaide in 1977. When I was three we moved to Clear Lake, a small farming community in country Victoria with a population of around one-hundred-twenty people, to be closer to my mum's sister. Clear Lake had a school and a church, so the forty-minute drive to Horsham was our hub for shopping. The country life is amazing. I have great, great memories of riding my bike to the neighbours who were a few hundred meters away, going to the creek in our backyard to build a raft with my brother, digging for beautiful old bottles, and horse riding with friends. I loved visiting the shearing shed during shearing season and doing all things farmy.

At age four I started prep at Clear Lake primary school with the other two prep children. The entire school had one class consisting of nine children, which was a vast difference from grade two of a school of around six hundred when we moved back to Adelaide for one year.

The coming years saw another visit back to Adelaide for a two-year stint. Going from farming life to city life didn't bother me. I always went with the flow and

CHAPTER 4: Sharron Keating

made friends easily, probably much like I have all of my life. One of the positive by-products of moving around so much is that I really embrace change. I do adjust well to going to new places and meeting new people. I suppose for some it could have been unsettling, but for me it wasn't.

I loved being involved in everything. I think it used to annoy my mum a little, because I was always announcing the next thing I was going to try. For instance, a part in an Italian play, even though the only Italian I knew was counting to ten, netball, gymnastics, and plenty of other random activities. I just didn't like missing out on the action. If school requested students to try out for anything, I was there. Not that I was good at everything, but I had to give it a go.

We moved back to Horsham in 1989, and my brother and I attended Horsham Technical School. I was in Year 7, and he was in Year 9. I stayed until halfway through Year 11.

You became a hairdresser at one time and were quite successful. Tell me more about that.

All of my life I wanted to be a hairdresser. Being so sure of this, I probably didn't try as hard as maybe I should have at school. I had no desire whatsoever to go to university. It was hairdressing, and that was it. My parents were always supportive of anything I wanted to do, and they instilled a great work ethic within me. They suggested I volunteer at a salon if I wanted any chance of getting a hairdressing apprenticeship. Our school had a work experience program in Year 9, in which all students participated. I went straight to a salon and asked the owner if I could work there for two weeks for work experience. I absolutely loved it and offered to work Thursday nights after school and during school holidays. Soon after, it became a paying job.

At fifteen, I had three jobs. I worked at the salon, at Fossey's, and in a Jewellery store. I just loved working, and of course the money it brought me. Every boss I had in the early days was tough, fair, and expected a lot. I'm grateful to them all, as they too had a part in shaping who I am today.

During Year 11, I read an ad in the local newspaper for a hairdressing apprentice. I thought all of my Christmases had come at once, as they were very few and far between. I remember rushing over to my neighbour's to type up a résumé, because we didn't have a computer. Amongst my nerves, I had a real confidence that I would get the job. I focused on all of my accomplishments that would put me ahead of the other applicants. A few days later my name was called over the loudspeaker at school. I went to the school office where Mum was waiting, and she told me I got the job. I went to my classroom and shared the news with my friends. Then I packed my school bag and left. That was a great day. The start of my dream job.

I was halfway through Year 11 when I started the four-year apprenticeship. The following four years were certainly character building. It was a tough environment at times, and it really helped me grow into a strong woman and fantastic hairdresser. I acquired great training skills, since we were all required to train people coming up under us. At age eighteen I was teaching the first year apprentices.

At age twenty I bought a salon. I partnered with a lady I had previously worked with during my apprenticeship. Being so young, I had to learn a lot very quickly. Going from an apprentice to owning a salon was quite an experience. I sold my share of the salon to my business partner seven years later.

What made you leave hairdressing?

Owning a salon at a young age was a challenge. I didn't have any business maturity, so many lessons were learnt that I couldn't have gotten otherwise. More than that, it was a journey of learning and discovery. The courage to go into business at such a young age has helped me get to where I am today. But after seven years I was feeling really stale and felt there was more I wanted to learn.

I did lose the passion for it. I was so caught up in the *busyness* of being a hairdresser and salon owner, that I didn't challenge myself. Even though I learnt a lot through my mistakes, I rarely attended trainings in business or hairdressing. As Ray Kroc said, "You are green and growing or ripe and rotting." I certainly was ripe and rotting. At the time I didn't realize just how important it was to continually learn, and the end result was a feeling of boredom and emptiness.

It was also during this time though I decided to make a comeback to singing. I hadn't sung for over ten years. Lisa, a talented singer and musician who taught me to sing at church in my younger years, had started teaching at her home. I decided to take lessons and brush up on my skills. I would travel out to Lisa's

CHAPTER 4: Sharron Keating

farm house every week for the next two years. My goal was to sing at events with my boyfriend, Mat, the man of my dreams who I went on to marry. He played acoustic guitar and also sang. We would practice every night until late and went on to renovate our shed into a music room.

We called ourselves *Déjà vu* and went on to sing at many local events. Our first gig was for the eighteenth birthday of my business partner's daughter. From that we got another gig, and it seemed at every gig thereon we would get more and more bookings. I remember those first few gigs were so nerve-wracking. It was nearly enough for me to pull the pin. However, our desire to do well, and the pure enjoyment we got out of it, far outweighed the nerves. It was such a great test of self-belief. The confidence I gained from feeling the fear but doing it anyway would serve me well in years to come.

After I sold my share of the salon to my business partner, I went on to work for friends of mine who owned a boutique jewellery store. I managed the shop for five years, and I loved being a part of a team where growth was valued. I took some short courses in gemmology and diamond grading and learnt how to design and quote. Engagement rings were my favourite! Working with couples to design the perfect ring that would be handed down through generations was an exciting prospect. The culture was based around becoming the best version of you. I had the opportunity to train consultants who sold jewellery for the business in other towns. It was a positive place to work, and I was encouraged to read books on personal development, sales, and attend leadership seminars and workshops. I was like a sponge, soaking it all up.

During that time, I got married to my wonderful husband, and a year later we had our first son, Jobe. I decided to have a year off work. I'd been working full-time since I was sixteen, and I was thirty by the time I had Jobe. I wanted to be the best mum I could. Of course, I didn't quite make it a year, but I came close. I went back to the jewellery store a couple of days a week.

My husband's passion was to own a café, and in 2009 we bought Café Jas in Horsham, in partnership with his mum and dad. At the time I didn't have any intention of working there, and that lasted about two weeks. Mathew was soon calling on me to do a few shifts here and there, and it soon became apparent I needed to take on a role at the café. I left my position at the jewellers and concentrated on being a mum and contributing to our café. I worked on the floor to start with, as I wanted to learn all of the ins and outs. That's where I was needed, and customer service has always been my thing.

One month into the business, Mat's mum was diagnosed with ovarian cancer. Surgeons performed an operation, and she started chemotherapy soon after. She was travelling along okay, and we were told that with treatment she could survive for five years. After digesting the shock, we were optimistic and decided she would be fine. The chemotherapy knocked her around, and she had some good days and some not so good. Ten months later she was experiencing abdominal pain, and a blood test showed renal failure. She was taken to Ballarat for further testing. What we thought was just a precautionary visit and nothing too serious, wound up being quite distressing.

Mat's older sister lives in Melbourne. She has a strong medical background, and after visiting her mum she called us that night and expressed her concerns that it was probably only a matter of months, not years. We were shocked. We'd been so optimistic about her prognosis. The next morning we awoke at six a.m. to the phone ringing. It was Mat's dad asking that he and his younger sister get in the car and drive to Ballarat. They got to Green Lake only ten minutes later, when they got the news she had gone to heaven.

That must have been so hard on you and your family.

The tragedy of losing someone so close was the hardest thing we've ever had to go through. Seeing the man you love, lose his mum and all of the heartbreak that goes with it was excruciating. Mat's mum was a loving, nurturing woman who always put her children first. She worked hard, and her grandchildren were the light of her life. We were seven weeks pregnant when his mum passed away, and thankfully we had a chance to tell her. She was so excited for grandchild number six.

Ovarian cancer affects around twelve-hundred Australian women each year and about eight-hundred women die. Eighty percent of cases occur in woman who are over fifty years old. As women, it's so important to be in tune with our bodies and know what is normal for us. Go to your doctor with anything unusual or persistent. With all cancer, treatment is most effective when found and treated early. Ovarian cancer is often not detected, as symptoms can be disguised as "that

CHAPTER 4: Sharron Keating

time of the month" or menopause. Maybe even a tummy complaint or a digestive problem. Common symptoms of ovarian cancer are: persistent abdominal bloating, appetite loss, unexplained weight gain, constipation, heartburn, back pain, frequent urination, abdominal/pelvic floor pain, and fatigue. I urge all women to seek advice if you notice anything that is unusual for your body. Please don't wait.

Did you continue to work at the cafe?

Yes. The first few years I worked on the floor, I loved being with the customers, working with the team, and learning all of the ins and outs. In 2012 we decided to engage a business coach, and to this day he's still our coach, as well as a great mentor. He sat down with us, and together we set some great goals. That's where things really improved for us. We decided I would take on the role of marketing and events coordinating, a position I loved learning about.

I had no previous experience with marketing, but I got help from experts and studied up on marketing tips. It's been so rewarding. Events coordinating is another aspect I absolutely love. Starting from nothing but a few ideas to creating memorable occasions for our clients really lights me up. Mat is passionate about good quality food. He's forever watching food shows and researching the latest food trends. Our mission for the café is creating a genuine and unique experience our customers will tell stories about. We want our customers to feel like they're among family. That it's their home away from home.

What are some of your struggles, and how did you get through them?

In recent times we had a situation within our business that I struggled with. I didn't really cope too well. It shook me up, and I'd never felt like that before. A beautiful friend of mine, Kirsty, who I've been friends with since we were children, suggested I read *The Alchemist* by Paulo Coelho. I'd never heard of it, but she kept encouraging me to read it, and I did a few days later.

She knows me so well. It was exactly what I needed at the time. What I learned from the book was that every challenging situation that comes your way is a time when great personal growth can happen. You can choose to learn and grow from it or feel failure and suffer. The book reminded me to stop, fill up my tank, and arm myself with some great tools to move forward. It was this challenge that gave me the clarity to move forward with something bigger and better.

When a challenge arises, it's a great opportunity to reassess and learn something new. At the time what I originally thought was this horrible, stressful situation was soon turned around. I asked myself, "What is my big why? What am I here for? What impact do I want to have on the rest of the world? What do I want to do for the rest of my life?" It made me think about me, I suppose.

I came to the realisation that even though I loved the café, it was very much my husband's passion. At that point we had two boys. The youngest was three. As a mum, sometimes you feel selfish thinking about yourself, but after reading the book, I felt I owed it to my kids, my husband, and myself to be the best version of me doing what makes me happy. After all, how can I raise my boys to be exceptional young men who are strong, resilient, and compassionate, if I'm not congruent with my own values?

I pondered all of these questions for two months but still didn't really have clarity around what I was going to do next. I was continuing to keep this all inside when I met with my business coach. It turned out to be the most uncomfortable conversation I'd ever had with him, and that's exactly what I needed. He challenged me, and I started with the excuses about how I didn't have the time to figure out what I wanted to do, because I was so busy working at the café and being a mum. He said, "If you really wanted to know, if it's really important, you would make the time to work it out."

We made a list of my strengths and things I love to do, and after doing some homework he'd set for me, I remembered an important conversation Mat and I'd had more than ten years ago in which we decided to write down our goals. He'd written down that he wanted to own a café, and I wrote down my desire to mentor people. It hit me that I'd gotten so busy with life and kids that I'd stopped thinking about what I wanted. Why is it that when we become mothers, we forget about our own dreams and desires and feel selfish if we do? It was from that moment on I started to think deeply about *Who am I? What do I want to do? What legacy do I want to leave?*

Within two weeks of the meeting with our business coach I had enrolled to study for Master Practitioner of Coaching. I would wake up in the mornings wanting to read and study. I'd go to bed far too late, because my head was is in the books. Once again I was green and growing. I felt inspired. On the first of July 2015, I launched Epicure Coaching.

CHAPTER 4: Sharron Keating

What is the goal of Epicure Coaching, and what advice would you give to those who've lost their way?

The goal of Epicure Coaching is to help people who feel stuck, whether it's in life, in business, or within their team, and they just don't know how to move forward. I help them change those patterns and create a new way of thinking, so they can grow and develop, because the problems they have now are caused from their old way of thinking. Behavioural profiling is a tool I use to help teams and management communicate effectively and identify gaps within their teams.

When you help someone and see them transform their lives, it's an amazing feeling. It starts with drawing a line in the sand. Then it's about getting clarity, knowing how to set goals, changing what you focus on, and seeing a clear outcome.

Movement is clarity. Wishing, hoping, and waiting will never give you clarity. It doesn't matter which way you move, just go. Once you start, you will gain more clarity. No matter how busy you are or not, you'll always wonder if you have the balance right. It's about awareness. If you notice there's an area of your life that needs improvement, then work on it. Your life is a work in progress. Keep striving to be the best at whatever you do.

I strongly believe that women, especially, can work out what their true passion is. There's the saying that if you find your true passion, you'll never work another day in your life. Who wants to be in a boring old job, just making ends meet? It takes up such a huge part of your life that if you're not enjoying what you're doing, it impacts on everything else. It's difficult to go home and be upbeat and happy. I would encourage women to work out what it is they really want to do. A great way to start is by making a simple list of all the things you love and all the things you're good at. What do you value?

What are some of your personal challenges, and how do you maintain balance?

There are the occasional moments when I feel like I'm not doing my best, especially when it's a busy time. I worry my family is suffering. I love what Tony Robbins says about creating magical moments. He says you can be a parent who has a lot of time with your children and not really be present, so when things get a little crazy it's about making those moments magical. All of my decisions are based on sustaining, nurturing, and serving my family. Joy and family are my top values. It's hugely important that within my family, within our business, there's an element of joy. Every time I leave my house I think about what I can do to make someone happy. Little acts of kindness are what make the world a better place. If everybody, every day, did one little thing to brighten someone's day, think about how much better and simpler the world would be. Mark Twain said, "Kindness is the language which the deaf can hear, and the blind can see."

How important do you feel mentors are?

It's so important at any age and any stage of your life to have either a mentor or coach challenging you. The best of the best all have someone pushing them along. When I speak to students, I encourage them to find someone who's doing what they want to do and ask them to be their mentor. These people have filtered through what doesn't work. They've been there. They've done it. They don't bother you with all of the rubbish. They just give you the good stuff. I think a lot of younger people, in particular, are too nervous to ask. When I was young I figured I was just a school kid, and nobody would want to be my mentor. It's so untrue. Many people are flattered to be asked.

Would you share some quotes that are inspirational for you?

My favourite is by Maya Angelou. "Try to be the rainbow in someone's cloud." Tony Robbins said, "Only those who have learned the power of sincere and selfless contribution, experience life's deepest joy: true fulfilment." And finally, Oprah Winfrey said, "The biggest adventure you can take is to live the life of your dreams." What I think this quote is about is spending the time to think deeply about what you want to do and put it into action. Believe you can do it, and go for it.

CHAPTER 4: Sharron Keating

cafe Jas
LICENSED BAR AND RESTAURANT

Café Jas

Café Jas is a thriving Horsham coffee shop that provides everything from a relaxing coffee to an inviting meal or a professional catering and functions service. Since Café Jas opened in April of 2000, it has grown significantly to cater to the culinary needs of the Wimmera. Our café is licensed, and we have wheelchair access and ample parking.

Café Jas is a popular meeting place where you can relax and enjoy an afternoon or morning tea with quality fresh-roasted, single-origin coffee extracted to perfection by our amazing baristas using the Synesso coffee machine. You can select a meal from our breakfast and lunch menu where you will find plenty of local produce, including sensational olives from nearby Mount Zero. We pride ourselves on our strong set of values that our fabulous team delivers to our customers each and every day. Our team provides a cheerful, genuine, efficient, and professional service to make Café Jas feel like your home away from home.

Our welcoming café seats up to seventy five, with your choice of alfresco or inside dining. It's the perfect venue for a corporate function or to celebrate a special occasion such as weddings and birthdays. We're also available for private, evening functions. Your menu is prepared by qualified chefs who can cook up anything from a sit-down meal to canapés. Enjoy any style of function in comfort and style.

Café Jas provides Horsham residents and the surrounding communities with a professional and reliable catering service. Our qualified chefs will design a menu suitable for any occasion, and we prepare the food at our café. You can choose to call in and pick up your order, or we have a delivery service that will bring it right to your door, along with qualified wait staff, so you can totally relax. But why not drop in and indulge in some of our delicious menu items delivered with friendly and stress-free service? We also have a fantastic range of gourmet condiments to select from for your own cooking adventures or as an ideal gift.

Our Mission at Café Jas is to provide a genuine and unique experience our customers will tell stories about.

Epicure Coaching

Sharron's passion for exceptional customer service, love of the hospitality industry, and desire to help businesses create dynamic teams is the origin of how Epicure Coaching was born.

Sharron brings with her the passion to create dynamic teams working together to deliver the company's vision, mission, and values. This is done by working with business owners, managers, and teams through one-on-one sessions and group trainings. Sharron uses a behavioural profiling tool that identifies an individual's behavioural type.

CHAPTER 4: Sharron Keating

Some of the many benefits of using behavioural profiling in the workplace include:
- Learning your strengths
- Strategies for improvement
- How to effectively communicate with other types
- How to retain quality staff
- Identifying gaps within teams

Each type of staff has specific drivers, and if you meet those needs, they will stay. Behavioural profiling and human needs psychology used together is a powerful way to discover the individual needs of your teams. Visit www.epicureoaching.com.au to join our mailing list for regular tips, ideas, and insights.

*"Turn your wounds
into wisdom."*

Oprah Winfrey

CHAPTER 5

Eva Sifis

CHAPTER FIVE

Eva Sifis

Eva is an artist, advocate, and survivor. After a career as a dancer, she now produces community arts and has just enjoyed a return to the stage. Her wish is to highlight the fortitude and tenacity that lies latent within all of us.

I first met Eva at a leadership workshop organised by Leaders of Tomorrow CEO Aaron Mashano. Eva sat next to me. She had a certain glow about her, and I wanted to hear her story. She'd gone through so much in life yet seemed not to have a victim mentality. She shared her vision of how she wanted to empower people who had gone through some of the trials she'd been through. Eva is a remarkable young lady, and I look forward to seeing the impact she will make on the world.

Tell me about your early life

I've always been creative. It's the core of my being. The first born of three children with Greek heritage, I grew up in the Adelaide hills. The community there nurtured my individuality. Foraying into the arts from a young age, I went to a small hills primary school, afterwards receiving scholarship to a college. The social dynamics amongst the girls overwhelmed me though and after two years I decided to leave. This uncomfortable situation with peers was mirrored at the next two high schools. I strove to further my experience of production and performance throughout those days, setting me up for what was to come.

Did dance help you to fit in? What was it like travelling the world?

At last it felt as though I had landed on my feet when I entered the dance music scene. Here was a community of people with similar motivations. We were a big group of malcontents bonding through the electronic dance music breaking completely new ground. I managed collectives made up of fellow ravers with the right moves. We would dance at clubs and dance-parties. In 1996 the newest club opened in the city. I immediately went to see when they would need stage

CHAPTER 5: Eva Sifis

entertainment. Our company got the job and the chance to be paid to do what I love has been a driving force ever since.

Taking on an opportunity to dance in Japan, I celebrated my twenty-first birthday there. As a reality far removed from anything I ever could have imagined, when I look back, I realise that is an age when you are invincible. Living in a different country I embodied the essence of what it meant to be *me* for I was free from any history. The connections I made with others, residents and travellers alike, were pure in a way I had never before encountered.

I performed four separate residential cabaret contracts overseas before moving to Melbourne. There I danced at nightclubs and worked as a host, roller-skating around discos with a girly troupe wearing cheekily inventive costumes. During study at a dance studio, I heard about an audition for a pop group. The intention was to live and perform in China. I jiggled with anticipation. On track towards a life similar to my Japan days, I passed through the auditions and entered rehearsals.

Then, as I crossed Nepean Highway after one of the first practices, I was hit by a car.

What happened then?

Nobody saw the accident happen, but the couple in a neighbouring car heard the impact. The lower half of my right leg was snapped. The tight, elasticated boots I wore flew off my feet and as my hip hit the car, my feet swung up around me and came to rest near the windscreen. My head hung over the edge of the bonnet. After being carried forty metres, the driver's brakes caught the road and, with my body flying forward, my skull slammed to the concrete. I rolled under the front of the now stationary car.

It wasn't until the witness put their hand on my throat to check my pulse that I started to breathe. A dark and rainy night, the ambulance took thirty minutes to come. They had to resuscitate me twice on the way to hospital. When I arrived, my leg was immediately operated on. I was put into an induced coma for it was thought the trauma would be too much for me to cope with otherwise. With no ID on me it took the Alfred Hospital ten hours to find out who I was. Once contacted, my parents took the first flight out.

Four days later the blackout-inducing drugs were stopped, but my coma lasted nearly a month. The doctors didn't have much hope for me. They warned my shell shocked family and friends I might never wake. Dad kept thinking they didn't know his daughter.

When I finally came to, it was with a long, drawn-out word beginning with an 'F'...

It must have been strange to lose a month of your life and still have a long climb back. What did you do?

It was suggested the time had come for me to be moved to Adelaide, however whilst unconscious, options for my recovery had been investigated. The best rehabilitation for people with head injuries was found to be at Epworth Hospital in Melbourne. Deciding to close his painting company in order to shift states to look after me, Dad worked cleaning at the hospital at night, grateful he could be close. A wheelchair was my transport for eight months as I learnt to walk, to talk, to negotiate stairs, to swim and even to run again.

Wrapped in intensive rehab, time passed. The broken connections in my head gradually found ways to join. After 18 months, when Dad started driving me crazy like he always used to, I knew I had begun to reclaim my Self from the void of Acquired Brain Injury.

But you must have still had a long rehabilitation process ahead of you.

Yes. We moved back to Adelaide where I could live independently. I'd had such a rich time creating a new life elsewhere that I felt in my gut a sense of resign. I love Adelaide, but for me it was a cloistered environment where in the past I had found it difficult to gain ground.

I reminded myself that I was only returning until I was better.

Lo and behold, once I landed, I fell into a black hole of services. Nobody knew me. I remember my raw frustration when, after some weeks marked only by lack of action from health services, I, along with my doctor, organised my rehabilitation team. This consisted of a neuropsychologist, a psychiatrist, a neuro-physiotherapist and an occupational therapist.

CHAPTER 5: Eva Sifis

Living with my unconditionally accepting cat in a tiny flat in North Adelaide, I would catch taxis to numerous appointments. When not seeing a doctor of some sort, I visited a gym walking distance from my house. There I focussed on classes that taught awareness of the body, like yoga, Feldenkrais and Pilates. These classes remain part of my rehabilitation even today.

Once a week I would walk a considerable distance to volunteer in the shop of an environmental organisation in the inner-city. Giving me camaraderie, purpose, and support, I aligned myself to sectors of the community I was interested in through volunteering. It eased me through my reintroduction to social skills as I was virtually a blank slate in that respect.

At that time my walking was stilted, my left leg flailing out at the hip with every step. I walked everywhere, forever concentrating on the movement of my legs. Waiting for taxis was a great chance to practice. Trying to walk in a straight line following the concrete blocks of the pavement, I would carefully place my feet beneath me.

Improving my gait became an eternal pastime. Never ending focus on my improvement gave me purpose.

Were you able to keep in touch with your dancing friends? Did you know anyone in Adelaide?

My social circle had once been varied and extensive. Having fun and partying is the way of life when you're young and experimenting with new things. However I found, once I could no longer enjoy these activities, the people I'd called my friends left me. Every one of them. This was extremely difficult. I was only twenty three when the accident occurred and treasured the concept of friendship. The sense of loss was carried for many years.

In Adelaide I had mates from earlier times and they welcomed me. For this I'm eternally thankful. When I look back, I realise at times I behaved in ways that were quite embarrassing. Due to the damage to the frontal lobes of my brain, my ability to censor my actions had disappeared. I'm mortified by things I said and did but can forgive myself.

I was a child again in so many ways.

I've likened my recovery to a graph with different levels of my psyche maturing at different rates. At one time I could mark where I was within the deepest sense of my consciousness by which childhood home I thought I lay within after awakening during the darkness of the night. What I identify as the 'I' aspect of myself has watched the 'Me' aspect develop through to an adult consciousness. It has been such an empowering, enlightening experience.

What other options did you seek besides traditional rehabilitation?

Once the time for seeing doctors and therapists had passed, I explored different modalities of healing like kinesiology, reflexology, Reiki, bodywork, and traditional Chinese and Ayurvedic medicines. These therapies are profound. I could sense and feel their effect.

In my opinion Western medicine can help you reach a certain level, but the focus is mainly physical. My experience shows there are many alternative options that can be consulted to help in recovery.

Antidepressants were prescribed whilst I was still in hospital. Never given a choice, the medical profession deemed my physical rehabilitation most important. It was assumed I wouldn't handle the grief that came with my trauma. Four years later and tired of not feeling emotions, I took myself off the high doses of antidepressants. When contemplations of suicide began, I realised I should have brought the dosage down slowly. Impetuous behaviour like this is typical with head injuries of the frontal lobes.

Taking a lower dose made coming off antidepressants possible. Being free from them for over twelve years now has emphasised a message at my core: *I need to feel to heal*. There is a place for antidepressants, but I fear people are losing touch with themselves because of the absence of their emotions.

What were some of the lasting effects?

I had 'post traumatic' epileptic seizures up to ten years after the accident. Big ones taking me to hospital in an ambulance, sirens blaring. Each seizure seemed to be instigated by light flickering on or emitting from the paper/screen from which I was reading aloud. I envisage a short circuit in that particular connection between my synapses. Anti-seizure medication in my daily pill dose contributed

CHAPTER 5: Eva Sifis

to my feeling of drugged mindlessness. I feel the time for seizures has passed now; that my psyche is no longer in emergency mode.

Physically, my disability affects my balance and coordination. Remaining conscious of my feet at all times, my left foot has to be reminded to flex before it's placed down. The dancer in me remains grievously dismayed by a body that doesn't remember how to move. Yet I dare to feel excited for possibilities obvious with small changes continuing. Learning to move all over again has been a challenge keeping me committed to gym classes. An interesting observation I found being during the rare periods in which I pushed weights, my ability to walk smoothly actually decreased. There is a contraction of muscle natural to this form of conditioning. I find by returning to classes that encourage proper functioning of the muscles I keep improving.

The injury has shifted my reality, causing my focus to be different.

The lasting grief I felt caused tears to flow freely and often. I observed the effect on people around me and felt ashamed. I felt like a switch flicked when any strong emotion came up and it caused tears to well in my eyes immediately. Thankfully this reaction has subsided with time. There is a great release of tension with tears. I wonder whether this is, in fact, a survival technique of sorts.

I remember practising reading and writing again after losing the ability. Handwriting is a fine art, difficult with lessened coordination and about fifty-percent sensation in my right arm. Before mobile phones had a calendar function, I would carry a little diary to record my many appointments. It was similar to those I'd bought overseas as a souvenir. Overjoyed to find the same designs for sale here in Australia and because they were so small in size, I learnt to write in tiny script. This is still a quirk of mine.

Were you still involved in the arts?

After moving back to Adelaide, one of my first ventures back into the arts was taking part in a program where I was mentored as a disabled artist. The mentor assigned to me was a younger dancer who'd only been performing for a relatively short amount of time. It didn't sit well with me. I was struck by the thought, *What can you teach me?*

My ego had begun to voice its indignation. A saying I used to repeat was that "when my head hit the road, my ego got left behind". My time as an innocent reborn was remarkable where I even lost my streetwise speech and the habit of swearing. As the years passed though, I was happy to have my spark start returning. This was most evident in situations that reminded me of my life before the accident. There were many intense occasions as I played with fire by stepping into the arts world again.

That mentoring initiative morphed into a project assistant role at the lead organisation for disability arts in the state. It was there I started learning how to write grant applications. Little did I know how much I would need that skill in the years to come! A successful application funded my research of the strong disability arts community in Melbourne. After visiting numerous companies, upon return to my hotel each night, I would write about my day. In five weeks I wrote 22,000 words. That's a quarter of a doctorate!

I've often said that I have a Ph.D. in 'Getting Better'.

A relationship was fostered with a Victorian disability arts company in those early days. I give such kudos to the manager. He kept in contact with me in Adelaide, nurturing me from afar. There was even a time we went to Sydney to hold a party at the Opera House where I met someone who would be a future mentor.

How were you able to merge your talents?

Back in Adelaide, my skills were consolidated to produce a series of circus skills workshops for children with and without disabilities named 'Roll Up, Roll Up'. I feel the best way to quell harmful preconceptions about people with disabilities is to experience being kids together. In the search for fun, new skills can be learnt, laughter can ring out and perhaps those ideas will never be formed. The facilitators of the classes showed the children that we're all essentially the same. The concept of ability is a perception. Circus gives options to all.

By chance, I met the director of an international youth arts festival held in Adelaide. Visiting a cafe in the Festival Arts Centre, all of the tables were occupied. When I spied a gentleman seated at a table with an empty chair, in my usual 'disinhibited', post-injury style, I asked if I could join him. After introductions were made, I brought up my project. The director liked it so much,

CHAPTER 5: Eva Sifis

Roll Up, Roll Up was included in the program for the up-and-coming festival. I was excited.

Alas, funding was hard to come by. During the year I studied Community Development, I would chase silence and the ability to concentrate, by visiting the library in the evening to apply for grants. Throughout that time I applied for five or six. With such a meaningful and important project, I didn't understand why I was repeatedly unsuccessful.

I bought a ticket to Canada. My intention was to stay with a friend I knew from when I worked in Japan. The promise of that adventure is what had motivated me to study Community Development as this training could have translated to possible work. Maybe a new life awaited me? I looked forward to the future.

But this is where your life took another turn. What happened?

The trip and Roll Up, Roll Up were fast approaching but I found myself gradually deteriorating. I couldn't breathe at night whilst trying to sleep and my face would swell round and puffy. Each morning my eyes became slits that wouldn't open for hours. I'd been going to the same gym for years but when I lay there on my mat having huge coughing fits, great rings of space opened around me. People thought I was contagious.

I didn't know what was going on. I kept going back to my doctor telling him something was wrong. He was frustrated, he couldn't figure out how to help me. When I was introduced to the Ventolin puffer that's used for airway difficulties like asthma, I stared at it incredulously. I knew inherently it was not going to help me.

Easter break began in a burst of sunshine and I went for a walk along the beach with my mum and my sister. Before long I had to find somewhere to lie down and rest. As I tried to breathe clearly, mum asked in a worried voice if I wanted to spend time at their house. Living alone at the time, I decided it was best to be around people, so I agreed. I lay on their couch drifting in and out of sleep. Since I'd already been to the doctor so many times in the past weeks, I groggily rejected going to the hospital to waste hours sitting in the waiting room and left it until the next day to see my doctor. I lay in a semi-conscious state until then.

Upon awakening in the morning, I was shocked to find spider veins popping up on my wrists and ankles. At the doctor's office and not thinking clearly, I remember asking how I could treat them so they wouldn't be noticeable. My doctor urgently advised me to go straight to Emergency as I may have had glandular fever.

After many scans, I spent a sleepless in hospital night due to the steroids I was injected with. They helped reduce the swelling so blood could get to my brain. The next morning, my doctor walked into the room. In my mind's eye, I can see him sitting at the end of my bed as he gravely told me, "Eva, there's a high possibility you have Hodgkins Lymphoma."

So with one month to go until I celebrated the tenth anniversary of my accident, I was diagnosed with cancer.

My parents came to my bedside and we sat in a silent state of shock. The oncologist arrived wearing an almost disbelieving expression as he flicked scans at the window to display the size of the tumour. It stretched from the base of my larynx in my throat to the top of my liver, pressing tightly against my lungs and heart. This is why I couldn't breathe. The enormous swelling left just a five mm hole in my trachea. No wonder my face was so swollen!

So, you had to go through a second recovery process?

It was said I needed urgent chemotherapy, and though I agreed, I wanted an alternative. A naturopath was seen as well. The natural therapy eased my ride through those challenging months and I believe it hastened my recovery. In my experience, both forms of medicine can be consulted in order to treat the whole of the body and person.

Drinking fresh-squeezed beetroot, carrot, celery, apple, lemon, and ginger juice up to two or three times a day, I kept myself going. Years before I'd learnt how this mixture cleanses the liver. I feel this was an important inclusion to my diet, as two times a month for four hours my body was infused with the highly toxic chemicals that make up chemotherapy.

I left the little flat and moved into my family's home for that year. This marked my third childhood. I am forever thankful my parents were able to look after me. After six months of chemotherapy, I was depleted. I'd lost weight. I lost most of my hair, my eyelashes, my eyebrows, everywhere. The freedom I felt after

CHAPTER 5: Eva Sifis

shaving my head in hospital mystified me. I felt the weight of years lift away. Empowerment is found in the strangest places!

Mum was my rock throughout this journey. She accompanied me to every chemo session, to every appointment with doctors and to the naturopath. I'm reminded of the bond a mother shares with her children. This was made real to me when, in the year after my challenge, Mum had a routine scan and a small lump of cancer was found growing in her breast. It was removed and we're all thankful. I remain blessed with the testament of a mother's love and devotion.

How did you climb back a second time?

For the year spent in recovery, I lived in a small home, blessed in company by two cats. They coloured the long days with their personalities.

My world darkened. Isolated and disconnected from life, I felt the spaces stretching all around me. After a highly successful festival season, Roll Up, Roll Up was picked by the government to be run in a primary school. But even with this success, by the year's end I knew something had to change. I was uninspired and life felt stale. So, after declaring myself as close to 'better' than I'd ever been, ten years after returning to Adelaide, I treated myself to the ultimate Valentine's Day gift and moved back to Melbourne.

It's been a slow and steady process. Upon first arriving, I acted in community theatre to give myself grounding. Gaining a position as an associate director of a film festival by and with people with disabilities widened my horizons. Following this formative time I familiarised myself with the entrepreneurial mindset through a network of businesses. Then, after that valuable experience, I returned to the arts and took on two mentors.

What followed was a dedicated period of working hard to achieve some important accomplishments. I developed a keynote speech of my story and enjoyed a return to the stage in *Embryonic Zombie Butterfly*.

This is what I named my autobiographical theatre piece as those are the words that slipped from my lips when I described how I felt in this process. I'm in an embryonic part of life, I've returned from Death's grasp, and yes, I'm still a butterfly. The season went astoundingly well. Watching the footage afterwards had a powerful effect on me.

I realised I had never lost that flame that was mourned so intensely.

How has your experience helped you reach out and help others?

Presently I'm building my experiences into a program called 'By Accident'. Currently being developed as a series of workshops, the program is intended for people moving away from acute care after a traumatic injury. They will have reached a level of recovery where hospital can't take them further. I hope to help others buffer the gap I experienced in my rehabilitation process. Out in the everyday world again, I did not feel prepared after leaving intensive rehabilitation to face a world so changed. My offering will make others aware of strategies and tools for coping with an enormously changed life.

The arts are something I would like to bring to By Accident. I can see it giving participants an opportunity to reach inward processes in a way that can't usually be accessed. Utilising therapies of expression may help assimilate new ways of being and give those feeling cut down the chance to participate in their evolution.

After a head injury, it can be difficult to process words on a page, so I'm proposing the use of theatre to bring a measure of understanding for the journey ahead. I found strength by consciously moving away from the western medical belief of the finality of head injury. Instead, I monitor the actual effects upon my being. The discoveries I've made have led to ways that have helped me for dealing with a forever changed perception of life.

What would you like to share with others who may have gone through similar traumatic experiences?

A key message of mine is to trust in your own guidance and use it to move into your power. It helped me to step away from the belief that only others know what's best. It's important to continue learning for your own insight.

Power is within everyone to heal themselves. Healing is not dependent upon specialists or drugs. Strength can be found within the self to go forward and seek alternatives. I've always tried to stay positive throughout this experience, even when my situation seemed hopeless.

I was a dancer in a wheelchair.

CHAPTER 5: Eva Sifis

A view I would like to share is to see trauma as the doorway; a chance to become aware of the ability to shape ourselves. I feel that we, as a society, have forgotten the basics of what it means to be alive. There are so many distractions capturing our attention that what it means to just *be* seems to have been lost.

Believe you will overcome.

Spirituality has been an important part of my journey. Brought up dazzled by Greek Orthodox ceremony due to continuance of tradition, with strength leant to my developing beliefs by eclectic spiritual studies. I acknowledge the divine aspect of all of our lives.

In my search I visited an ashram near Chennai in India. After a month spent training and taking part in ancient ceremonies, I have been blessed with brief periods of utter silence during my meditations. This is something I nurture during my daily practise. There are many benefits to dedicated meditation. The effects seemed small at first, but I find that it helps me to overcome sleep difficulties and contributes to overall calm throughout my days.

How important do you feel mentors are?

I could not achieve everything I have without mentors. My way forward is reflected in the statement, *Rest in the arms of your community*. As women, over the ages, our lives have revolved around community. But I sense in this increasingly individualised world, our hearts are crying out to be a part of something. I see us all now flying in formation, utilising each other's wind streams. That is womankind. Each on an individual journey, our formation has a purpose. We can help each other fly.

Remember, even superheroes have sidekicks and they are strong in their own right.

Where do you go from here?

It's taken sixteen years to reach this point. Each of those years has been required in growing the new me. Through all of my experiences, through all of the pain and the loss, I acknowledge it has all contributed to my genesis.

I remember standing at the fateful crossing on Nepean Hwy at the same time of night, one year after the accident. Imagining jigsaw puzzle pieces falling out of the sky, I saw that each of these pieces correlated to coincidences. When taking my first steps in life again, coincidences peppered my days with regularity. I remember being so blown away by what seemed like signposts hinting I was headed in the right direction. Ever since then, I see each experience or occasion that brings me further progression as a falling jigsaw puzzle piece. The pieces are creating a path leading to my future. There is quite a way to walk, but knowing I'm on the path laid by my own actions bolsters my steps.

To leave the comfort and dependability of life in Adelaide in order to come to Melbourne has shaken my foundations, encouraging new growth. The benefit of holding out my hand for assistance has been realised over a long period of time. Whilst still in the foundational state of learning everything over again, I totally depended on others. Now, instead of coming from a place of dependence I come from one of strength. I realise that nobody can do it on their own. It's okay to admit you find it difficult lifting the load.

From 2004-2006, I studied Wholistic Wellness. It spoke to me of areas left wanting in my exhaustive psychological treatment. I gained much insight and identified facets of the self I had never before touched upon. I also learnt a physical therapy called Human Transformation. This is deep bodywork that can reach all of the way into the muscles that line the bones. The treatment can cause cathartic change. Whilst in training, tears poured from my eyes when my right bicep was worked upon. Feelings of fear, grief, frustration, and anger all came to the surface. This led me to realise that coma memories were held there. Impact memories lay in my right hip and with that bodywork I experienced a flash of the car hitting me.

Our bodies, even our hair, hold memories. It has been so empowering realising that there's a bigger reality.

The journey of head injury has awakened me to Me. After all of these years of struggle I realise I am grateful. I feel absolute privilege in making my own decisions not feeling reined in by society and I awaken every day determined to follow my dream. There have been remarkable places inhabited throughout my long recovery. Each person's journey is individual, yet I have insight from which others can benefit.

CHAPTER 5: Eva Sifis

Embarking into business with open eyes, a fully utilised network, and an eager grin, I go forward an awareness of self-care. After all, up until now I've lived my life in accordance with the all-consuming, 24/7 reality of 'getting better'.

So many facets of my being have been explored through this experience. After expanding my view of capabilities both new and re-found, I've become aware that we're fluid beings. I'm intent on always improving. Likewise, a head injury can be a chance to look upon the world with a clarity that may have not been available before. It gives a raw set of circumstances in which it is possible to create oneself anew - to birth yourself using an adult consciousness.

To that end, I'd like to talk about what I call my second birthday. Sometimes my actual birthday wouldn't be honoured for years. I've never been one to throw my hands to the rafters on that day and say, "Celebrate me!" However, the date of the accident, May 15th, is one I want to honour. I just love it for it marks my rebirth. It's my *re-birthday*! A marker of the opportunity given to me to take conscious steps in my own evolution.

You've gone back to performing with* Embryonic Zombie Butterfly. *What made you want to perform again?

I had refused to dance after the accident. There's a disconnection from my brain to my feet, resulting in me not being able to coordinate or control them to any effect. Stepping back on stage with *Embryonic Zombie Butterfly* has shifted me by giving me a platform to embody and express my experience. Even though my body moves differently to that which I was once accustomed, the fire that burned through my previous life has been reignited. The standing ovations reassured me I'm still a performer. Acknowledging the artist within has been powerful and I intend to keep developing my performance.

What is your vision for the future?

My vision for the future is for people to realise the inherent oneness of us all. With the understanding we're each responsible for our own perceptions, great things are possible. Belief in the self is vital. Believe in that person standing next to you. Believe in the community. It's about faith. Here I refer not strictly to the concept of a Higher Power but to that fire within lighting your way. Your own little hurricane lantern.

In enabling those who have suffered traumatic injury the chance to see the freedom gained through their experience, I wish to unveil the opportunity they have to remodel themselves. I would like to help others see there is great power in taking the reins of your own recovery and stepping away from being packaged by someone else.

I'm a strong believer in action. I dream it, I see it. I couldn't live my life any other way.

There are three things that have driven me.

One: every time something bad happens I stop and remind myself to go "onwards and upwards".

Two: I remind myself in hard times that "this too will pass"; and

Three: is to keep living my life knowing things happen "for a reason, a season, or a lifetime".

CHAPTER 5: Eva Sifis

By Accident

byaccident.anewyou@gmail.com

St Kilda Luna Park Rollercoaster Photograph - Keith Persall

"Just to reassure you that there is a life after ABI. It may be a rough ride, but you just have to try and be positive about it. Just hang in there. It's like a roller-coaster, it's a rough ride but it's worth it."

~Warren Phillips, By Accident™ interviewee

After being hit by a car in 1999, Eva Sifis sustained severe Acquired Brain Injury. Everything had to be learnt again: walking, talking, interacting, and so much more. Following her exit from the hospital system, she embraced many years of rehabilitation and self exploration. Physical and cognitive systems had to be renewed and her entry to society occurred while developing basic skills lost due to the injury. As a professional performer, Eva already had insight into what the human body is capable of. This experience has strengthened her faith in the fortitude we all have. She had to call upon this fortitude to overcome Hodgkin's Lymphoma in 2009.

Fierce & Fabulous ~ The Feminine Force of Success

Life throws all sorts of challenges. How will you respond?

By Accident™ is being developed to support those entering new lives after traumatic brain injury. Informed by personal experience and mirrored by two percent of the Australian population, after the acute stage of rehabilitation there comes a time where the enormity of what has occurred becomes clearer. Our current system of post injury care does little to prepare a person for the world that lies ahead.

Brain injury can take all sorts of guises, irreversibly altering life to a version unlike the one lived before. By Accident™ is a short series of workshops for people facing the challenge of Acquired Brain Injury; with additional training for those in support roles. The effects of such a life-changing event are felt by everybody close to the injured party. Informed awareness can make the transition less overwhelming.

Having strategies in place and tools on hand for negotiating an altered experience of the everyday will help. There are many aspects of existing in our society that have to be considered when starting again. By Accident™ will focus on ways to approach this situation.

Now standing on the far side, Eva brings her unique experiences to By Accident™ with a depth of understanding that is unprecedented. Peer-initiated communication of knowledge such as this is extremely rare, and in the time following ABI, can provide a sense of solace and community.

Eva Sifis will offer By Accident™ in 2016. The initial email for more information is byaccident.anewyou@gmail.com

www.byaccident.com.au is coming

CHAPTER 6

Jacinta Petrie

"Every human is an artist. The dream of your life is to make beautiful art."

Don Miguel Ruiz

CHAPTER 6: Jacinta Petrie

CHAPTER SIX
Jacinta Petrie

Jacinta Petrie is the Founder and Chief Empowerment Officer of MPowering You. She's dedicated her life to empowering others by challenging and supporting them to take little steps and actions towards creating their inspired, authentic, and extraordinary life. Her amazing story of transforming her mono-polar life battling constant suicidal thoughts, self loathing, and emptiness inspired her to help others. She's helped so many find love for themselves and open their eyes to possibilities of the extraordinary. A life that is their divine birthright.

Jacinta and I met at one of Benjamin J Harvey's workshops. We went to dinner, and she came with her own organic salt. I figured someone this dedicated to eating healthy must have something important to share abut life. Jacinta has a big heart, and she cares for everyone she meets. I'm fortunate to call her my honorary sister, and she was a great help through a personal tragedy. We sat at the Foundation for Young Australians in my favourite red booth to do the interview.

Is there anything you'd like to share before we get started?

For over fifteen years, I battled with depression and myself. Now my story may sound like it goes back and forth and jumps around a little, but this is the nature of depression. It robbed me at times of coherent thoughts. It jumbled up my thinking and some of my timelines. In a way, I guess it was my mind's way of helping me cope. I promise if you stick with me, I will give you a happy ending worthy of any great love story.

Steve Jobs said, "You can't connect the dots looking forward, you can only connect them looking backwards. So you have to trust that the dots will somehow connect in your future. You have to trust in something: your gut, destiny, life, karma, whatever. Because believing the dots will connect down the road will give you the confidence to follow your heart, even when it leads you off the well-worn path."

My story is a bit like that. There is never just one thing in isolation that causes you to lose yourself, and there is never just one thing that brings you back. It's only looking back that I could join the dots and see how one thing led to another. My journey required constant vigilance, observation and reflection, and being completely honest with myself about who I was and where I was. Anything less would be delusional and a distortion of the truth, as well as a complete disservice to myself. I had an unrealistic expectation that life should be all love, support, and roses, with no challenges to my reality or thoughts. So to help you join the dots, let me share some of my life experiences and help you gain insight to my story and me.

Tell me about your early life.

I grew up in a place in Brisbane called The Gap. As a child I was pretty, bright, bubbly, and out there. I had a strong sense of myself and how the world should be. My mum, bless her fuzzy little cotton socks, thought I would be this great leader, organising the other kids and showing them how things were done. Instead I became quite introverted. Starting school was a pretty rude awakening. I'm not sure that I was made for sitting in a classroom and following all of the rules.

I did enjoy the social aspects of school up until Grade 3. There was an incident over some lollies, which was followed by me being cut off socially. Even at that early age I had a strong sense of what was right and wrong and stood for truth and justice. It was a theme that would underpin my struggles and challenges in the years to come. I cannot honestly say if the lollies were the cause or not. What I do know is that because I didn't give this person what they wanted, I would pay a high social and emotional price that came in the form of bullying.

The reason I share this memory is because I believe this is when I realised I was different. I didn't seem to fit everyone else's model of the world. This was also the beginning of me turning down my light and probably the first mask I wore. I placed my heart behind a wall, and over the years that wall would grow thicker and harder. I wasn't going to be hurt or betrayed like that again, or at least that's what I thought. It was also when I started trying to fit in and please people in an attempt to fit in and be accepted.

While I struggled to fit in at school, I found a horse down the road from my best friend at the time. It was in the paddock lying under a fence and barely able to

CHAPTER 6: Jacinta Petrie

move. Her name was Abbey. I raced home and told my Dad. He's a big man. Six foot four. A big, solid bloke who I saw as not too emotional. But I could see on his face his heart melted when he first saw Abbey. A bond opened up between us that day, and it wasn't long before Dad had bought Abbey for me.

There's another childhood memory that shaped my life. Across the road from our house was a creek. It had rained heavily, so the water level was up. My brothers, sisters, and I liked to get on tyre tubes and ride down the creek. I can't remember what made my sister and I attempt to go down the creek without a tube, but we did. Less than a hundred metres from where we took off, we were pinned against a pipe, with the water crushing me against it. I couldn't breathe properly and started to panic. I thought I was going to drown. Lucky for us, a stranger came along. He shouted for us to let ourselves go under. My sister did and was free. But I was so overcome with panic, so paralysed with fear, that the stranger had to physically force me down and under the pipe.

Did you get into trouble as a kid?

When I reached high school, I tried to exert my independence. I was the wild child. I broke the rules and always got caught. While I didn't mean to, I caused my parents much distress. I was fiercely attempting to assert my independence and managed to choose the most challenging ways to display it. Looking back, I would say my parents were saints.

While my friend's parents were away, we got into their alcohol cabinet. By the time I left I was pretty inebriated. By some miracle I succeeded in getting my horse home and fed before I passed out in the middle of the street. I ended up in hospital where they administered charcoal to assist me in absorbing the alcohol. My dad didn't talk to me for weeks. His approval was so important to me. I felt like I broke his heart and that he would never trust me again.

I felt like a terrible, wicked person who was not worthy of her father's love. The wall around my heart was starting to thicken, and the self loathing started to creep in. I was really starting to struggle with who I was and where I belonged in the world.

What were your hopes and dreams?

I wanted to be a teacher, but I wound up leaving school halfway through Grade 11, when my English teacher shattered my dreams. I failed on the English paper I had written. I approached her with the view of getting feedback. The words she said to me are etched in mind forever. She said, "I hope you don't ever want to be a teacher, because with these marks, that will never happen." I did want to be a teacher, but in that moment I took on the belief that I would never be one, I couldn't write, and I would never be good enough. I gave my power away that day. Don Miguel Ruiz, in The Four Agreements talks about the power of words. He says words are magic. They can be used to create good, or they can be misused and cause great damage.

How did this experience change your path in life?

I went to my parents and told them I wanted to leave school. After much tussling, they agreed so long as the following year I would do a secretarial course at a well-known, well-to-do Catholic school. I agreed.

But when I told my fellow students what school I came from, they rejected me. From then on, they called me names and physically abused me. They were relentless in deleting my assignments off the computer and alienating me. My spirit and self-esteem took another battering. All that mattered was doing my best to survive. And survive I did. As part of the course, after the first four months you could start applying for jobs. I was successful at my second interview, and I was over the moon.

On 2 June 1986 I started my job in the electricity industry. I think by that stage, I had compartmentalised my friends to meet certain aspects of myself with little crossover. I figured this way if one set of friends didn't work, it wouldn't flow over into any other friendship groups. No one person truly knew me.

The good news is I flourished in the electricity industry. I was respected and accepted by my peers and fellow workers. By the time I was eighteen I had a great bunch of friends I used to hang around with in and out of work, as well as two terrific male friends, Giovanni and Brad. Life was good.

CHAPTER 6: Jacinta Petrie

You eventually went into the Army Reserves. What happened there?

At nineteen my best friend talked me into joining. It was there I met the guy I thought was the love of my life. Within three months I became engaged. One year later he'd disappeared out of my life, never to been seen or heard from again. I was totally devastated, not to mention confused, hurt, and bewildered. We were so connected. It wasn't until later that a friend told me he'd slept with my best friend. The same one who got me to join the Army Reserves. Ironic.

How did that experience affect your future relationships?

Somewhere around the age of twenty-two, I started to develop deep and strong feeling towards Brad. I knew deep-down he was my forever after. By this time we were best of friends, and for years I hid my feelings. At the age of twenty five, Brad came to me and told me he'd met a girl and was ready to get married and settle down. He asked if I could see myself settling down with him, and if not he would pursue this relationship. But I couldn't let the walls down around my heart and let go of my fear, so I watched my best friend and true love soul mate get engaged to another woman. From that point, I shut down and concentrated on my career in the electricity industry and the Army Reserves. I became quite masculine and guarded with my emotions.

There was a brief moment when Giovanni and I could have connected as something more than friends, but when it came down to it, he was just as fearful and guarded as I was. That unfulfilled moment destroyed our friendship. My world was unravelling, and my emotional shutdown was complete. My heart was closed for business. For over ten years I medicated my feelings for Brad with food, alcohol, and sad songs.

Tell me more about your professional life.

In 1997, I was made redundant from the electricity industry. I was devastated. I loved my job and the people I worked with. By 1998, I had found a job in the Queensland Government in a supervisory role in the records section. My dad was stoked, since it was important to him that his children were in good, safe, and secure jobs.

My days of being in an industry and a job I loved were over. I had a staff member who became obsessed with me. He would swing between staring at me with puppy-dog eyes and harassment. One time he screamed at me with such aggression to f*** off. I nearly wet my pants with fear. Then I laughed. I remember thinking I finally I had something I could go to my supervisor with, but they put it down to a difference of opinion. I reeled. How could my manager not see what was going on?

I was so trusting I didn't believe people like him existed. I took on the belief it had to be my fault. I moved work areas shortly after this and it would be some time would pass before our paths would cross again. After seeing my photo in an industry publication, he sent an email with a veiled threat. The department did an 'investigation'. This led nowhere, and they wound up blaming me. This was the beginning of my downhill slide. I started to withdraw from the workspace and friends. In the space of twelve months I'd put on nearly thirty kilos. It was like being in an abusive relationship. I felt dependent on my weight to keep me safe, secure, and hidden.

By chance, I was lucky to be offered a job in another area within the department. For the next year I worked in relative peace. As recognition for my knowledge and skills, I was asked to join a records project within the division. I was excited and thought finally things were on the up and up. Wrong!

There were two women in charge of the project from the business development area, and they were nasty pieces of work. For six months they spoke to me in the third person. After I offered a suggestion in a meeting, right in front of me one of them would say, "I'm not sure Jacinta fully understands or comprehends what is required here," to which the other would respond, "I'm sure that if Jacinta did understand what we meant, she would not have said that." For nearly six months I put up with this, and management only did something when I put in a medical claim for a locked jaw I was suffering due to the stress. Eventually these women were removed from the project, and I was given responsibility for running it.

That sounds terrible. Why did you stay, and how did it affect you emotionally?

Why would I stay in a job like this? I had low self-esteem and no self worth. Who would want me? My job paid well, and I had a mortgage. There was also a part of me that said, "Stuff You! I'm not going to let you beat me."

CHAPTER 6: Jacinta Petrie

It was during this time that depression set in for the long haul. My thoughts became toxic and self-abusive. Feelings of being alone, isolated, and unlovable consumed me. I started hiding away in my home and had limited contact with people.

After the records project I moved to an area that was involved in disability services. I loved this job but not my manager. After working there for a couple of months, I realised her thoughts were less then coherent and that she had a drinking problem. She would edit everything I wrote. After I would make the changes and re-submit, she would re-edit again. One time this happened thirty-five times. It reinforced what my English teacher had told me and eroded away at my self-confidence. My toxic thinking and suicidal thoughts spiralled out of control.

I punished myself for any moments of happiness I experienced. I beat myself up mentally and convinced myself to take myself out. I didn't give it much thought or planning. I found some prescription pills and downed them with a bottle of bourbon. Then I put myself to bed and waited for the end to come. This was on a Monday, and I woke up on Friday still alive. As I tried to think of other ways to end the pain, the phone rang. It was my friend Cheryl. She reached out and touched my heart and soul. I may not remember the words, but I do remember the kindness and sincerity. I returned to work after five days. Nobody had noticed. It was like I didn't exist.

In 2004, I was thinking of going back to school to get the grades to become a teacher. My mum had read this article about a mentoring program that combined property investing with universal laws of prosperity. I did not hesitate. I signed up for the nine-month program.

In my gut I knew this was my ticket out. I was going to be a property millionaire, happy and free from working at a job. It would set up the foundation for the rest of my life. Things didn't quite unfold as I had imagined, but it was a year of exponential growth, learning, connecting, and discovery.

During those nine months, I went to see a psychic and card reader who was part of the group. At one point during the reading she stopped and told me I needed to find my feminine power again. She also asked if I practiced self-love. She meant it in a sexual way. I was taken aback by the question and answered with a resounding no. Any love I had for myself ended ten years ago when I'd let Brad walk out my life. But I did listen to her, and as strange as it sounds, it began my journey to self-love.

Sometimes during our journey of self-discovery, we lose friends along the way. I understand this happened to you.

Judy and I had been friends for seventeen years. We did nearly everything together. We were as thick as thieves. It's only looking back that I realise our relationship was a co-dependent one. We kind of needed each other to feel valued. The same year I started the mentoring program, Judy and I went on a holiday to Victoria, which is a southern state in Australia.

While we were staying with friends, the lady I was joint-venturing with was negotiating a property purchase in Brisbane that required my friends to drive me into town to a real estate agent. I also signed up for a course in property investing in America, so I had to use their phone at one in the morning, which I was told was okay.

The day before we flew back to Brisbane, Judy and I stayed in the Melbourne city, so we could go on a guided bus trip to see the Great Ocean Road. She'd hardly spoken to me that day, so that evening I asked her what was wrong. She insisted it was my snoring that kept her awake. It wasn't until a couple of weeks later that I asked her what the real issue was. She said I was rude to the friends we had visited, and they felt used by me.

I had a coach at the time, and I told her about this. She said to ring up those friends and make restitution, but they said they didn't know what I was talking about. That I was an absolute delight, and they were happy to help me. So it turned out Judy had the problem.

I was moving forward with my life, and Judy didn't like it one bit. I was de-layering and on the journey back to me. In the end, I decided to let the friendship go. When you begin to grow and change for the better, there are people who need you to stay down in quagmire with them. Sometimes you need to let them go in order to grow, change, and develop. You can't help anyone by staying there with them.

CHAPTER 6: Jacinta Petrie

Did your situation at work improve?

In 2006, the manager who'd rescued me from psychological abuse in the disability services area had now become abusive himself. He had a new boss who micro managed and pushed all of his buttons, so he took out his frustrations on everyone else.

One time as he stood over me and screamed, I was paralysed with fear. The air constricted, and my brain swirled. The next day on my way to work, I suffered my first panic attack and couldn't go in. My first thought was to go to the doctor and get on stress leave, but the doctor's approach was to give me pills and tell me to go face my fears. I did end up going to work, and for a while things were okay. My manager seemed remorseful until it happened again, this time in front of many people.

I called the work counselling service. When I went in and explained what was happening, he gave me a choice to book an appointment with a psychiatrist before I left his office, or he would have me committed to a facility, because he considered me a high suicide risk. Lucky for me I had a friend who worked in the field, and she recommended a colleague of hers who turned out to be this lovely, caring, supportive physician. After she listened to my story, she asked me how long I'd been off work. When I said I hadn't, she put me on stress leave immediately and said she could not foresee me going to work for at least six to twelve months.

I broke down in that moment. For the first time someone had not only listened to me but believed me. Work had become my whole reality. I think part of it was I couldn't figure out how to fix it. I liked to fix things and can't stand to be defeated.

But that kind of stress doesn't just go away. How did you deal with it?

For the first two or months off I barely existed. My panic attacks were ongoing and triggered by having to leave the safe zone of my house. A friend of mine came over and dragged me to a personal development seminar. For the first time in months I felt like I'd be able to get rid of my toxic thoughts and feelings and start living my life again. That was enough to make me walk up to the sales counter and sign up for their six signature programs.

The next two years were game changing. My first course was Neuro-Linguistic Programming (NLP). The best way to describe NLP is that it helps you get out of your own way long enough to find solutions or negate negative experiences and emotions. The second last day of the course I began having panic attacks. It was also two days before I had to go back to work.

I volunteered to do a process on stage that was called parts integration. It's a technique to overcome bad habits and creates harmony between parts of the unconscious mind, so their values are in alignment. A person with integrated parts is more congruent, empowered, and clear in their decisions and actions. For me the two conflicted parts were security versus freedom. I had to realise that security was in my freedom and that freedom was not in my security. This was the realisation I had at the end of the process. My panic attacks stopped, never to return.

That's great. Did it have an impact on your work situation?

It took me nearly six months to realise it was the workplace that was the problem. The people were toxic and saw nothing wrong with their bad behaviour. I went back to work and made my peace with my manager. Underneath, he was not a bad person. I was transferred to another area and put on a return-to-work program. By that time I had applied for a job with a twelve-month contract, and when they offered it to me, I took it. It meant I had to resign from my job, and I took great pleasure in handing in that letter.

I would hold many jobs after that, but one thing was clear. I was not made to work for government departments or permanent work. I challenged people's thinking and paradigms just by being me.

Do you have stories to share about female empowerment?

I was practically begged to go to a striptease course. I was well over a hundred kilos, still hiding out in my house, and feeling unattractive. I could no longer look at myself in the mirror. My first thought was, Hell, no. But being the good people pleaser that I was, I caved.

This experience turned out to be the greatest experience in divine feminine

CHAPTER 6: Jacinta Petrie

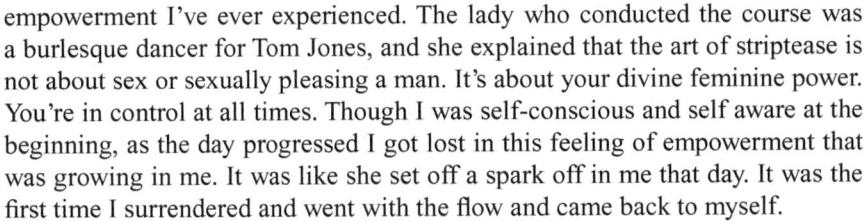

empowerment I've ever experienced. The lady who conducted the course was a burlesque dancer for Tom Jones, and she explained that the art of striptease is not about sex or sexually pleasing a man. It's about your divine feminine power. You're in control at all times. Though I was self-conscious and self aware at the beginning, as the day progressed I got lost in this feeling of empowerment that was growing in me. It was like she set off a spark off in me that day. It was the first time I surrendered and went with the flow and came back to myself.

It came time to do the final performance of our striptease. I had just started when I noticed that a passing gentleman stopped to watch me through the window. I saw it in his eyes and the expression on his face that he was completely captivated. I held his attention for the entire song and learnt a valuable lesson that day. There's nothing more captivating than a woman who stands in her own power.

Shortly after doing this course, I felt I needed to start taking some control over my life. One morning, out of nowhere, I was inspired to get up and start exercising. So at five in the morning I sprung out of bed and drove to my parents' place in Samford. On my first walk I recited mantras in my head and out loud like, *In twenty-one sleeps I will be fitter, healthier, and vital.* By the end of the twenty-one days I was walking fifteen kilometres. I had blisters all over my feet, but I didn't care.

I wound up dropping two dress sizes, and because I was feeling good about myself, guys became interested in me. In fact, I went out with a friend one night, and they were lining up to approach me. My friend met a guy, and he had a friend, a really cute Scotsman. We hit it off. He asked me if he could by me a drink and indicated we both go up to the bar. He fumbled to get money out of his pant pocket and accidentally dropped some on the floor. When I retrieved it, I did one of my striptease moves. He couldn't speak for a while afterward.

It was around this time I sought out another psychic card reader. She told me that the guy I was in love with at twenty-five was now single. She could have only meant Brad. I tracked him down and found out it wasn't true. He had a wife and two dogs.

In 2009 on my fortieth birthday, I decided to create a bucket list of three things I would do before my next birthday. I happened to be having lunch at the Greenmount Surf Club on the Gold Coast with a friend of mine, when I declared I would learn to surf.

I walked up to the instructor at the Learn to Surf van and said, "I'm overweight. I'm not flexible. I've only ever been in the surf up to my thighs, and I'm not a strong swimmer. Can you teach me to surf?" He said he could if I had the determination. My friend said I did. The instructor's name was Dan, and he had a sister named Jacinta. I have a nephew named Daniel. For me that was a sign. I told Dan I would be back during the winter.

A special bond wound up forming between us. I knew that connection was on a soul level. Dan taught me how to fall back in love with myself. When I was surfing I felt my connection to the gods and to nature. My senses where heightened, and I was alive, happy, and connected. It was a divine arrangement. As my surfing improved and my friendship with Dan grew, so did my confidence.

One day I was the only one who showed up for the group lesson. Dan gave my board a push and said some like "… and you're even more beautiful." It made me fall off my surfboard. I said "I'm confused, what do you mean more beautiful? How do you improve on perfection?" We both laughed.

On another occasion he said with some hesitation that other instructors told him I was in love with him. I confirmed it and talked about our connection. But I also said I would not sleep with him, because my love was pure and without lust. I could be me when I was around him. There was an openness and honesty I have never experienced with a man. We were, and still are, connected on a soul level.

In 2011 after the floods hit Brisbane, I was working for Community Recovery Centre with a bunch of great people. The girls took it upon themselves to do a makeover. They called it Operation Jazzie. It's my nickname. What came out of that was nothing short of a miracle. Next I tried internet dating. It's the best personal development program I've ever done. It showed all of the parts of me I didn't love and brought up my insecurities and fears. On the flipside, it allowed me to work on my stuff. I became more resilient, more vulnerable, and learned to fall back in love with myself all over again.

Tell me about when you decided to start eating healthy.

On the 28 December 2012, I ate my last Tim Tam. I was driving home one day listening to the radio, when I heard a man say, "If you can't afford to eat healthy now, then you need to be able to afford to be sick later." I had no kids and no partner. I only had me to look after me. If I didn't change my ways, I was heading

CHAPTER 6: Jacinta Petrie

for a world of hurt.

I had attended free talks about using wholefoods as medicine and about colon cleansing, so I set a date to start the colon cleanse and completely change my diet. I have never looked back. Over the years since I've done courses in wholefoods, raw foods, detoxing, cleansing, and fasting. I've learnt about health from a totally different perspective. My focus was not on losing weight but getting healthy. As a happy consequence, I lost weight and influenced many people to make healthy changes in their life.

Did you experience any setbacks, either in your personal or professional life?

After losing two jobs within a short period of time, I decided to let go of the place I was renting, pack up my life, and move to Melbourne for five weeks to do my version of the Eat, Pray, Love journey and maybe even decide what I wanted to be when I grew up, if in fact I wanted to grow up at all.

Things were going well. I was having all of these little adventures, when two friends of mine must have seen what was really going on and told me to rest. That's when I crashed. Then I cried and denied. Did some soul searching. Cried some more. Slept and slept. I spent lots of time on Facebook and signed up for a Visionary Leadership Conference from a friend's post. In the end I gave myself permission to rest and enjoy myself and to stop judging the process or comparing it to what I perceived I should be doing.

I went back to Brisbane for three weeks, so I could do a detox course. Then I flew back for another four weeks in Melbourne where the tears came again, then anger, then frustration.

How did you turn it around?

I attended a freaking amazing life-altering event. Sunday, 10 November 2014, will go down as the day that changed how I would perceive my life and experienced the world. I realised that living an inspired, empowered life from my highest values was no longer a choice but an absolute!

I found the vehicle to propel myself in the form of Benjamin J Harvey and Dr Demartini. Again, the gods had given me what I needed. I experienced a happiness that came from deep within me. At the end of the day I had this moment where my gratitude was infinite, sincere, and truly inspired. In that moment I was present to who I was and to the unlimited possibilities of what I can experience in this beautiful, wonderful, extraordinary life. For the first time, I knew I could have any life I wanted. I gave myself permission to dream and be inspired. To live life from my highest values and let go of all of my stuff. To be open to loving myself and others unconditionally, and date the destinies of my choosing.

Most importantly, I gave myself the freedom to live my life from my heart and soul. On the same day I attended the Visionary Leadership Conference, I met a lady who would help rid me of my suicidal thoughts.

How did she do that?

Okay, let's go back to 2012. I received a letter from my accountant. He told me I had to find $75,000 to pay back my self-managed superannuation fund. I was told I had to put my house on the market. Being compliant, I did. Even when the house sold it was at a loss, and there was a significant shortfall on the money owed to the self-managed superannuation fund. I was panic stricken and I started to go down that old too-familiar road. I wanted to die. When I was denied a bank loan I just snapped. So, there I was the day after my forty-fifth birthday, sitting in the Apple Store in Brisbane city, totally succumbing to suicidal thoughts as to where the best place would be to throw myself in front of a bus and get it over with.

The only thing that made me hesitate were the words Benjamin J Harvey said at the conference. "I was overweight, I was depressed and I was $130,000 in debt." I argued with myself and went around and around in my head. It was a real battle not to go find that bus.

While I was arguing with myself I got a message from a friend of mine asking how I was feeling. I told her what I was contemplating. She came to get me, and I explained how I felt totally stupid for the situation I had gotten myself into. Looking back, I understand there was a reason for all of this. It was so I could take responsibility for my life, clean up my mistakes from the past, and open up the way for the inspired life I had committed to.

On the 12 December 2014, I was chatting with the lady I met at the Visionary Leadership conference about what had happened and how I was in suicidal mode. She asked me to describe how I felt. I told her, and I became overcome

CHAPTER 6: Jacinta Petrie

with panic as I felt like the air was being sucked out from around me. I could hardly breathe. My world went dark.

She asked if I'd ever experienced being drowned. I told her I had, and she offered to do a process with me that would take me back to that event and clear the effect of it from my timeline and physiology. After the process was finished, not only did I feel a shift, I haven't experienced a dark or suicidal thought since. And I've experienced some tough moments since then. I was able to seek out a lawyer and another accountant to get me out of that mess, so I could take back control of my life. It took me from when I was eight years old to age forty-five to deal with that trauma of nearly drowning. It was like an epiphany. All of the dots started to join.

You promised a happy ending.

Yes. Here is the happy ending I promised. On the 22 January 2015 I decided to look up Brad on Facebook and much to my surprise, there he was. I thought twice about pushing the add friend button, but I put that aside and within hours he accepted. We chatted, I found out he was now single, and he ended up inviting me over.

Within half an hour, I was knocking on his door. He opened it, and my heart melted. There was the man I had loved for over twenty years, and my feelings had not gone away. I laid it all on the line. I told him how I felt about him, my vision for the future, and that if he couldn't see a future with me, I would walk away. He told me he could see us growing old together, and he would be the rock upon which I could build the rest of my life.

I feel like I'm the star in the greatest love story ever told. I had attracted my true love soul mate back into my life. He gets me at every level and supports and encourages me to keep going. He's the inspiration behind my heart-centred inspired business, MPowering You.

What is MPowering You?

My vision for the future is to be an inspirational leader, connector, creator, teacher, facilitator, organiser, speaker, and communicator. The vehicle for that is MPowering You. It was born out of my desire to inspire people to take action and build an authentic community based on self love, self care, self sustainability, and genuine connection. It's also about the creation of a farming community with a healing and education centre that focuses on connection back to self and others through the land and knowledge.

It's my deepest hope to create something I can be proud of leaving for future generations, so when people look back they see this as the time when people took back their power, and peace was created through self-governance and self-reliance. A time when we no longer work in concrete boxes as slaves to money and someone else's paradigm.

MPowering You is about dreaming big, starting small, getting your shit together, and taking the little steps and actions required to live an inspired life. I am your Support and Accountability Partner and the creator of the Little Steps programs.

If you want to know if it works, just ask Brad, who volunteered to undergo the thirty-day Little Steps program. Afterward, he went from eating toxic, fatty, fried, microwaved food to juicing daily and eating salads and green smoothies. He's much happier with himself, and his thinking is much clearer.

You've lived quite an amazing life. Do you have any advice for people who may be stuck?

If I had any sage advice to give it would this:
- Own who you are, and never give your power away.
- Stop trying to please people and win their approval.
- Remember that no matter how bad the world seems, every morning when you wake up it's a brand new day, and the sun will eventually shine.
- Love yourself first.
- Read the Mastery of Love, The Four Agreements, and The Voice of Knowledge by Don Miguel Ruiz.
- Do not, under any circumstances, let anyone tell you that you're less than perfect. You may be battle weary and finding your way back from a dark place, but you're still perfect.
- You have the power to change your life. All it takes is little steps and actions.

In the movie *Finding Joe*, they talk about an event that happens to get you to separate from the life that's not serving you and gives you a call to adventure. In some circles they say that if you're not living your true purpose or in accordance

CHAPTER 6: Jacinta Petrie

with your values, the universe will give you a tap on the shoulder. If you don't take heed, the universe will tap louder. And if you're still not listening, then the universe will send you something huge that forces you to wake up and go on something called The Hero's Journey, where you have to face your demons and slay your dragons. At some point you start to realise that the demons you're fighting aren't outside you. They're the ones inside. Then the hero, after conquering his or her demons, returns home with the gift, the treasure that is their story of how they had slain their demons.

In the movie, Iyanla Vanzant says, "It is important that we share our experiences with other people. Your story will heal you and your story will heal someone else. When you tell your story, you free yourself and you give other people permission to acknowledge their own story."

With all my heart, it's my deepest hope that my story has touched you in some way. And if you're not living your inspired life, please hear it as a call to action to be fierce and fabulous, and go out to live your inspired life. Take your hero's journey, and come back to share your experiences.

MPowering You

At MPowering You We Value
Learning, Community, Tenacity, Adventure,
Persistence & Humour

Eighty percent of people are living unfulfilled lives in jobs that do not make them happy, while dreaming of some great windfall that will magically make their life so much better. And I totally understand why.

CHAPTER 6: Jacinta Petrie

I hated my life, and I hated me. I woke up at the age of thirty five, single with no kids and a mortgage, and thought, *What the...?* I was stuck in a job I hated, being bullied and harassed. Weighing in at 115 kilos, I felt unlovable and worthless on the inside. I was depressed and suicidal. I couldn't see a way out and had no passion for life. In my head I heard myself saying,

"When I win the lotto ..."

"I can't leave work because I have mortgage."

"I want to do what I love, but I can't see how it will pay bills and the mortgage."

"Just one more course, and I will be ready."

"When I have all the steps, then I will start."

"I will start next Monday." [1]

I was lucky to have a wakeup call that came in the form of a complete and utter breakdown. It was this crisis that gave me back my life and a chance to get my shit together. I had to get off my arse, stop making excuses, stop procrastinating, and take responsibility for my life.

I invested in a coach and a lot of self-education.

I learnt that if you want different results in your life you have to do things differently. I had to find the courage and confidence to live life on my terms and conquer my fears.

I started taking action. I let go of my excuses and twenty-five kilos, attracted the love of my life from twenty years ago back into my life, and created my own business that just lights me up on the inside!

---

1   Monday is like that New Year's resolution that you set but never follow through on.

I'm now excited about being alive, and I'm determined to help people who want more from life.

Don't give up on YOU! And don't ever give up on your DREAMS!

Here is one testimonial:

Jacinta has an incredibly vibrant, supportive, and genuine energy coupled with an open heart and acute insight and ability to see where a person is at and asking the relevant questions for people to gain direction and clarity in the life – guiding them from where they are to where they want to go in their personal and professional life. Her gift is helping others move past their limiting beliefs that are holding them back and motivating them to take action in creating their desired life.

~ Hayley Turner, http://www.soulentrepreneurs.com.au

At MPowering You, we help people to confidently take action on their dreams, live a life they love, and feel great about who they are.

Start your transformation today by emailing mpoweringyoucommunity@gmail.com for your no obligation FREE Coaching Experience, or join us on our Facebook page, https://www.facebook.com/pages/MPowering-You

MPowering You to dream big, start small, get your shit together, and take action.

CHAPTER 7

Kia Dowell and Chantal Harris

"Injustice anywhere is a threat to justice everywhere."

Martin Luther King

CHAPTER 7: Kia Dowell and Chantal Harris

CHAPTER SEVEN

Kia Dowell and Chantal Harris

Kia and Chantal are professional keynote speakers, published business authors, accredited coaches, and leadership experts. They've worked hard to define the principles of The Cultural Connection Code while working with business and community leaders. They have an e-magazine, Pathfinders, that's thought-provoking and informative. They ask the hard questions and tell real stories about the change they are making by breaking down cultural barriers.

I first met Kia at the Follow the Dream program run by the Kununurra District High School. We'd been invited to inspire a group of high-achieving kids. Kia is a remarkable young woman with a strong cultural heritage. She's dedicated herself to improving the lives of others and making this world a better place.

I first heard of Chantal when I was filming with B Visual Media for the East Kimberley Aboriginal Achievement Awards. I knew she was passionate about social justice and was an active member in our community. I finally got to have a proper chat with her in Perth for the book interview.

I found these women fascinating. They both have one vision, and that is to change the narrative. They're doing just that by educating the corporate world.

Tell me about your early life and how you feel it's impacted on what you do today.

CHANTAL

When I think about what has happened to get me to where I am today, I would say it's a similar story to most people. A lot of it comes from my experiences early on in life, and they've guided me to make certain decisions that have led me down different paths.

My parents are from New Zealand, and they moved to Australia right after they got married and started their family. I'm the oldest child of four girls who was raised by my incredible mother. I grew up in a nice little mining town that was surrounded by cotton farms and people who had lived there for generations.

The town had a railway track that went down the middle of it. Generally, non-Aboriginal people lived on one side and Aboriginal people lived on the other. It wasn't until I got a bit older that I understood there were those who saw Aboriginal people as different in quite a negative way. As a child you just think people are people. Children have the beautiful gift of seeing similarities, not differences. I also figured out that even though Aboriginal people grew up and lived in the same town, had access to the same schools and facilities, and did the same things we did, their experience of growing up in Australia was often quite different from mine.

So I guess it was those early experiences that started me wondering why this relationship is so strained. It was almost like everyone was happy that Aboriginal people stayed on their side of the railway track and kept to themselves. I kind of got the feeling Aboriginal people weren't that keen to connect with the broader community, due to some really negative interactions they'd had in the past. The good news is that as a teenager I was lucky enough to go to an Aboriginal community. I had a good friend there and was able to stay with his family. This basically changed the way I experienced everything!

It was amazing to see the world through a different set of eyes. The wonderful experiences I had and was told about in this community weren't taught at school or shown on the news, that's for sure. It was then I realised nobody I knew had been in direct contact with an Aboriginal person, so everything I'd learned up until then came only from observations and opinions based on what they saw on the streets or in the media. Then they attached their own meaning to it and drew their own conclusions.

These "single stories" of Aboriginal people were passed down like folklore and created an unimaginable amount of damage. I think the most upsetting and shocking part for me as a kid was knowing these people were being seen in such a negative light. And here I was having these positive experiences with Aboriginal people who were intelligent and funny and kind and giving, so it was at complete odds with what I'd been led to believe by the people around me. Now, please don't get me wrong, I don't think they were bad people, but

CHAPTER 7: Kia Dowell and Chantal Harris

they'd been led to believe these misconceptions as well. It was almost as though it had been passed down through generations, and no one had bothered to check the actual facts.

I got to experience it for myself and wound up understanding that a lot of the issues people talked about weren't necessarily associated with circumstances that Aboriginal people themselves had created and had more to do with polices, legislation, basic human rights, and the unfair thinking of people outside of the Aboriginal Community.

I got a sense that perhaps the way we were looking at this so called "Aboriginal problem" was a bit backwards. I believe Aboriginal people know what's best for their own Communities and have the knowledge, strength, and resilience to do something about it. The only thing missing was having access to the essential economic resources.

Aboriginal Communities need funding because of decades of government policies that had prohibited them from being able to build their own wealth, while the organisations providing the resources would dictate exactly how the money should be spent. After my first trip to a Community as a teenager, I wondered how we could build an economic base for Aboriginal communities themselves to promote wellbeing, culture, and prosperity in their own way, without being reliant on outside resources. This was why I decided to pursue my Commerce degree and eventually set up our business, The Cultural Connection Code, later on in life.

KIA

I'm a *Gija* woman from the East Kimberley of Western Australia, a community called Warmun, otherwise known as Turkey Creek. As children attending *Ngalangangpum* School, my siblings and I would wake up, put on our little uniforms, walk to school, and learn *Gija*. I loved that the first thing I did every morning was connect to culture through language. I really appreciate the foresight our elders had to merge that balance between the Aboriginal and non-Aboriginal worlds. Everything we did was infused with *Gija* culture. Now we have opportunities to learn about the *Ngarrangkarni* (Dreamtime) stories and understand why they were important to spread to each generation. It was about seeing what can happen when both worlds coexist.

That grounded me. It still does. I only have to reflect upon those experiences to know how fortunate I am to have the life I do. In saying that, I must add that there were still some horrific and tragic incidents my family and I were exposed to. When I was around eight, a pregnant family member of mine was a victim of domestic violence, but as an eight year old I had no idea what to do with this information. I was too scared to say anything.

What ended up happening is that she got beaten so badly she almost lost the baby. That moment solidified in me an awareness that it was no way for a woman to be treated. This was my catalyst to consciously pay attention to the world I was living in. I wondered how it was I got to eat three meals a day, have somewhere safe to sleep, and protective parents, while other families, including those close to me in the community, were exposed to domestic violence, sexual abuse, and substance abuse.

When I was twelve we left the community, because there wasn't a high school. We went up to Darwin, and that was a culture shock in itself. We went from a school of almost all Aboriginal kids to almost no Aboriginal kids. We sounded funny, because we were speaking *Gija*, Kimberley *Kriol*, and English. I think about my younger siblings, who were fair skinned and light eyed, walking around with these funny little accents. Kids being kids, you know they were curious, but they could also be quite mean.

To help balance the high energy of raising six kids on her own, our mum put her foot down and said to pick one sport to participate in, so to begin with, we picked basketball. In terms of what basketball represented to me, it was an opportunity I didn't know was possible until I moved to Darwin. Up until then it was always just watching the Chicago Bulls or the Dream Team on VHS in the childcare centre where my aunty worked. My cousins and I would all gather around this tiny little TV, put the video in, and watch in amazement for hours. But I didn't know it was a possibility for someone like me, at least not until one of my coaches said, "Hey, have you thought about this?" It lit something inside of me I didn't know I'd wanted.

When I was twelve I tried out for my first State team and got rejected. I was so gutted, because I had tried so hard and did everything I could but obviously lacked the skills and basketball thinking to make it, so I did what any kid would do. I took the next year to commit myself to being the best I could and figure

CHAPTER 7: Kia Dowell and Chantal Harris

out how much I could improve. I even went as far as sleeping with a basketball in my bed.

It paid off when a year later I got onto the State team. From there it just snowballed. The next step was a national scholarship program, and as part of that program we were given journals to monitor and record what we ate, how many hours we slept, and what our goals were. I remember writing down four goals. One was to play basketball in America. I don't know how I came up with that, but I figured if Michael Jordan could do it, so could a girl from Turkey Creek.

I was just so naive at the time, but it was good. If I'd known how hard it would be, I probably wouldn't have done it. The next goal was that I wanted to wear the green and gold and go to university. My last goal was to own my own business. One of the reasons was that my dad has run his own business for as long as I can remember, but I also recognized that it was the most effective path to breaking the cycle of welfare dependency I saw as a child in Warmun.

So from the age of fourteen until I was twenty five, my life was all about pursuing those four goals and becoming the best athlete I could. By the age of twenty five I had achieved all but the last one. That's when I got a phone call from my grandmother and parents telling me it was time to come home and share my experiences and knowledge with my family and my community.

Living in the U.S. was an incredible experience. I got to teach people about Aboriginal Australia, and I'm pretty sure I was the only Aboriginal person at the University back then. But it was special, because there were young women who had left countries like New Zealand, Bosnia, Croatia, Lithuania, and Poland going through this experience of being away from family. We bonded so much that I now count them as my sisters.

Being in Texas and on the border of Mexico was a different experience. While at the University of Texas at El Paso, I enrolled in a unit called Chicano Studies. It was about the movement of Indigenous people and what it meant to be Chicano, Mexican, Hispanic, or Latina. That was an inspiring unit, because it gave me a lot to reflect on in terms of how Australia not only appreciates, but values, Aboriginal and Torres Strait Islander people.

I chose to pursue a degree in Business Management, because I was still fuelled by the disparity I saw as a child between my community and the multi-million dollar mine twenty minutes down the road. While there were some people, including my family, who had employment opportunities, I wanted to understand the role business could play in shifting the level of welfare dependency, so communities like mine wouldn't be forced to depend on government handouts.

We must look at communities for the strengths they have. While there wasn't an overwhelming opportunity for economic development back then, now there are opportunities that aren't being realised, including the development and investment in people. Human capital. This was something I was, and still am, deeply passionate about. It's why I made the decision to continue on with my MBA in International Business.

I recall that day so clearly. It was while I was in Turkey representing Australia at the World University Games (we won bronze!) that I had the opportunity to speak with some of my teammates about what it was like to play professionally at home. After considering their feedback, I felt it was clear that the best investment and decision I could make was in myself. So after we competed, I accepted an offer under an academic scholarship to further my study.

When I returned to Australia at the age of twenty five, I thought about what I'd been exposed to in the States. There just didn't seem to be that same sense of entrepreneurship or innovation, but we're getting better now. It's exciting to see the rise across Australia, and the world, as we use business to affect positive social change.

How do you incorporate the different cultures into your business?

CHANTAL

I think everyone can learn from the sophistication and intelligence of the Aboriginal culture and the way the rules are set up to make sure everyone looks after the greater good of the people around them. It has always been my personal belief that if we, as the collective Australian society, incorporate more of this philosophy into our schooling systems, our workforces, and particularly in corporate Australia, we'd all be better off.

CHAPTER 7: Kia Dowell and Chantal Harris

I'm constantly learning. There are so many times I'm amazed by the difference in my life when I start to look at the world in a different way. I need to be clear that I do not speak or teach about Aboriginal culture. It's not my place and never will be. However, I do incorporate some of the principles and protocols into my own life where I can. One of the values that Kia and I have for our company, The Cultural Connection Code, is *liaarn* which is a *Gija* word that loosely translates to heart-based, intuitive leadership, or leadership of the self and instinctual connection. I'll let Kia explain more about that.

KIA

When we work with our clients it's not just from the head space. It's about getting to connect with them at a deeper level. Once we connect at that level, that's when real change starts to happen. I think all human beings have it in some form. Our goal is more about reminding them what they can do and using traditional Aboriginal culture to give them examples. For instance, meditation. That's not an exclusively Aboriginal thing. In South Australia they call it *dadirri*. It's about mindfulness. We had a woman tell us that she's been to so many professional development courses and executive leadership courses in her role as a high-level executive, but it took her coming to our Female Leadership Advantage course to remember how amazing women are. You can't teach that kind of stuff, you can only experience it.

We have certain cultural protocols that are based on the fundamentals of *Gija* law and culture. It's about being able to incorporate ideas like the principles of our kinship system, which is based on respect for all things and all people. When it comes to women and the role we play, it's about seeing where we can influence positive social change by sharing our tools and experiences.

CHANTAL

Our company provides business and strategic consultancy, as well as a range of cultural capability and Aboriginal Leadership training and mentoring programs. What we've found in our experiences working with hundreds of people is that a lot of the "traditional" leadership programs that have been implemented in the last couple of decades have all been centred on intellect. We flip that and focus on intuition. Let's concentrate on just remembering who we really are and connecting back to that.

Some people don't find it an entirely comfortable experience, because they want specific course outlines and outcomes. They want to know exactly what's happening and what they'll get out of it. And for us it's not about the programs. We're here to facilitate an experience for people to connect back to a lot of what they already know is there but have covered up with all of these different layers, and give them a safe space to do it.

In a practical way, that shows up in our decision making. We always wonder what's best for the Community. Can we add value? Has it been done the right way? Have the right cultural protocols been followed? It's not about how much money we're going to make.

What have you had to sacrifice to achieve your goals?

KIA

We have absolutely made a conscious decision to sacrifice some of our social life. You feel like you're constantly saying no, but you have to hold on to that bigger picture and the ultimate vision of what you want. In saying that, let me add that you do have to remember to invest in your friends and the people who support and love you.

CHANTAL

I think it's about consciously making deposits into what I call the "emotional equity" bank. All entrepreneurs know you can feel so drained when you aren't paying enough attention to your social and family life, and it's just work, work, and more work. But there are times we would do this work even if we weren't paid for it. It just fills your soul with so much emotional equity. So what if I had to get up at four in the morning to meet a client? The payoff is incredible because of the work we get to do, the people we get to meet, and the experiences we have.

We're currently building something that's so much bigger than the two of us. It can be heavy sometimes, but other days we feel so fortunate to be afforded this opportunity and to have so much support. You don't have a business without clients, and we've had some incredible people who've trusted us and invested their resources in us. We will be forever grateful to those who went out on a limb in their own companies and worked with us. They've taken a risk, and we

CHAPTER 7: Kia Dowell and Chantal Harris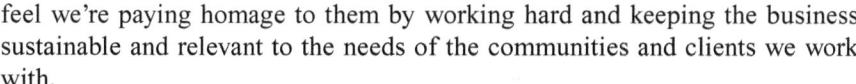

feel we're paying homage to them by working hard and keeping the business sustainable and relevant to the needs of the communities and clients we work with.

Where do you get your inspiration?

KIA

I don't have to look that far for inspiration. All I have to do is see young Aboriginal and non-Aboriginal people collaborating together. Or the stranger I witnessed giving a homeless person some money. A lot of times we get so caught up in the idea that it has to be this massive A-HA moment. It's the everyday miracles I look for, and in our work we're blessed and grateful to have the opportunities and the experiences we have, because we meet incredible people on a daily basis. Our family and our partners are a staple of inspiration to us.

How did you two meet and start your business? What is your mission?

CHANTAL

Our business started when I was working for a mining company over in Queensland. I'd just about finished university, and while researching for an assignment, I came across this man named Ian Trust, a respected Aboriginal man who had established the Wunan Foundation in the East Kimberley. I loved that he had a different perspective on what was happening at that stage in Indigenous affairs. So I went to the Wunan website, cut out a picture of their logo, and then hung it on the noticeboard in my little apartment I was living in at the time.

Within a few weeks, a job vacancy came up. I applied, got an interview, got the job, packed up my entire life, and was on a plane to Kununurra within two weeks. It was April Fool's day so I was ringing all of family and friends to tell them I was moving to Western Australia, and no one believed me, because everyone thought I was like mucking around for April Fools!

I didn't know a single person living in Western Australia, let alone anyone in Kununurra, but as fate would have it, Kia had left America and landed back in Kununurra that same week I moved to town.

KIA

I'd been over in the States for eight years and had some incredible experiences, but after that phone call from my parents and grandmother, I came back and had the chance to connect with Chantal through an event called the East Kimberley Aboriginal Achievement Awards. I was working for Rio Tinto's Argyle Diamonds in their Communities team, namely looking at Native Title Implementation. Chantal was with Wunan, which was the host of the event. Argyle was a major sponsor. Unfortunately, though in retrospect I suppose I should say fortunately, the coordinators who were in place pulled out at the last minute. That meant we had to pull it together in six weeks, when normally it takes six months.

As part of the nomination process and getting to know the incredible individuals and their communities, we saw what worked well and what didn't. We often spoke about what we could do beyond our roles, and that formed the catalyst for what The Cultural Connection Code is today.

CHANTAL

For me it was this incredible experience to go and live somewhere I'd never been before. By that stage in life I had travelled to Europe and most of Asia and the Pacific Islands, but I hadn't done much travelling in my own country. Having the courage to pack up and follow my dream allowed me the opportunity to meet Kia.

All of a sudden I had Aboriginal people who were like family. Kia's sisters became my sisters, and I was welcomed into the Community through my friendship with her. That is something not a lot non-Aboriginal people get to experience. I was not only going into these remote communities, but people were opening up their homes and including me in their lives and family activities.

It was such an amazing, personal journey.

Professionally, working on organizing the awards meant we got to meet so many great people in the community and the organisations that support development in different capacities. We had to work with a lot of large corporations and government agencies to pull the event together. It was a unique perspective to see how a community, the corporate companies, and government worked

CHAPTER 7: Kia Dowell and Chantal Harris

together. Like Kia said, we got a great understanding for what worked and what didn't.

There was a real theme of burnout and frustration among Community leaders. What was discouraging was that there was a Community with a specific set of needs and aspirations, and a corporation that could provide for them, yet even though there was much anticipation, years later almost no impact was made. Those who represented the corporations and government agencies had often moved on to other jobs, but the Community members were still there, and they remembered the hopes and promises made to them.

You start to wonder why that happens. Where does it fall down? What could be done better? For me, it was always about the role non-Aboriginal people can play to make sure the solutions, the initiatives, or anything else that could benefit the Community, are co-designed with the people who will continue to live in these Communities.

That's when we started to wonder what we could do as a company to make those with the resources understand that if they invested, it would be money well spent and could progress not only the economic development of Communities, but the social and cultural wellbeing of these amazing people as well.

The services our business offers are for both Aboriginal and non-Aboriginal people to create the learning, knowledge, strategies, and capabilities through specific tools for both sides to work together better. Our biggest hope is to see Aboriginal Communities thriving over the next fifty years and for the people to be healthy, happy, and in positions where they can create their own wealth, so they can make their own choices for themselves and their families. It's about getting the younger generation to understand the difference between Aboriginal culture and welfare culture, because they're two totally different concepts.

How do you bridge the gap between the non-Aboriginal and Aboriginal communities?

KIA

Growing up in Warmun formed the foundation for a lot of the work we do today in the space of cultural connection between Aboriginal and non-Aboriginal people who can leverage culture to accelerate business and leadership. We have programs like Pathfinders Leadership Program and Women's Circles, specifically designed for Aboriginal women seventeen and older in a variety of circumstances. Some are in prison, some are in University, and others are engaged in full-time employment. These programs will help them remember how incredible they are.

Someone once said we shouldn't call what we do leadership workshops but healing workshops, because for a lot of the young people who've been disconnected through culture or their families, it lets them know it's okay to be where they are on their journey of discovery, especially when it comes to their identity. They're just at a different place on their journey. We try to get non-Aboriginal people to understand a history they weren't taught, so they can be part of the solutions as opposed to perpetuating the cycle that until recently had little success.

For a lot of the non-Aboriginal people we work with, particularly established key decision makers, we tell them that part of their leadership and decision making must be founded in facts, not opinion. It's about understanding the influence and the role they play in making decisions once they have this new knowledge and awareness.

I believe that sometimes they have no idea, because Australia's true history and the experience of Aboriginal and Torres Strait Islander people hasn't been taught. Now we know that's changing with the new curriculum, which is fantastic, but it's not our role to make them feel guilty or sad or angry about it. It's to present the information in a way that shows them how much of an impact it has on their business. Then we teach them strategies and tools, so they can apply it in a way that's useful rather than a one-way delivery of information.

CHANTAL

As I've previously said, I never speak on culture or cultural matters. That's not my place. But what I can do in our business is to always ensure we have the right person with the right knowledge and endorsement from their Community for whatever region we're working in. It's always part of our design process in any project.

Like we touched on, a lot of our work is to facilitate a conversation that will bring a certain level of change. It doesn't have to be about people becoming

CHAPTER 7: Kia Dowell and Chantal Harris

over-sensitized to the issues and developing paralysation, because they think the problem is too big for one person to do any good. It's going to take a collective of consciously capable people to do this.

We talk about what we can all do in our individual roles that will create change. There are also people who want to take it all upon themselves to become the saviour of an entire race, which can be just as damaging. We're always concentrated on how we create positive progress,

I believe everyone can contribute in a positive way when they have the right knowledge to cultivate the right attitude, and are given the right tools to get the work done. At some stage we all have to move away from just talking and do something. That takes courage and a certain amount of risk. Our business ensures those risks are minimised. Some people have great intentions and want to help, but it's about being able to understand your role and how to help.... and just a hot tip: it isn't self-appointing yourself as a saviour of the Aboriginal race!

Tell me about your magazine, Pathfinders

KIA

We recognize we can't be all things to all people or in a hundred places at the same time. This has helped us shape our overall strategy. Part of our plan is to get our message out to as many people as we can. In order to do that, we created an online community that for the first two and a half years consisted of a monthly campaign of sharing and gifting lots of valuable content based on what we'd learnt or experienced.

Then one day I think I just got so frustrated with how much we were talking about "taking it to the next level" and said, "Let's just bite the bullet and do it. Let's start the magazine we've been talking about for the past three years." It was something we both committed to in terms of having a new platform that's engaging and entertaining, while also included something that would inspire us. It goes without saying that it was also a business decision to figure out who we wanted to include.

We wanted to do something different, something positive, and something to combat the negative news media we often see. That's where *Pathfinders* comes in. It's a process in terms of getting the publication out there, but the feedback from those who read it is that they're excited by it. It's centred on a strength-based approach as opposed to what we see often in traditional media, which is to focus on the negative.

CHANTAL

Pathfinders is an online magazine for business leaders, Aboriginal businesses, and people who want to create social change. It's for those who have the courage to take the risks and forge a new path in how the whole big web of "Indigenous Affairs" is approached. It's such a great tool, and it doesn't cost much to produce, because of advanced technology. It's all set up. People just go to our website, sign up, and a copy is delivered to their inbox each month.

The magazine started, because we wanted to find a way to share what we experienced. We've worked with around forty different clients over the last two years, and each of them brings a new element of awareness and learning. We needed to be able to get those ideas out and start sharing stories of people we work with and meet. We're able do that through the *Pathfinders* magazine, which is sent to thousands of people every month.

KIA

The people we profile may not get covered in magazines like *Entrepreneur* or *The West Australian*. We want to be an extension for what they're doing. And it will expand. At the moment our focus is on Western Australia (WA), but in the next twelve months we're looking to expand that reach as well.

What is your advice in regard to mentors?

CHANTAL

From a professional level it's always been really important for me to surround myself with people who have integrity and wisdom, and that we treat each other with mutual respect. I'm always nurturing and growing a circle of incredible individuals around me. I had to move away from some people and situations that no longer served me and my own mission. I'm always mindful of who I spend the majority of my time with. Who I'm listening to. Did they earn their own *street cred* by getting out there and doing it themselves?

CHAPTER 7: Kia Dowell and Chantal Harris

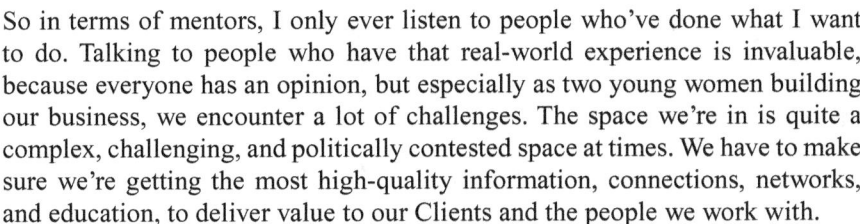

So in terms of mentors, I only ever listen to people who've done what I want to do. Talking to people who have that real-world experience is invaluable, because everyone has an opinion, but especially as two young women building our business, we encounter a lot of challenges. The space we're in is quite a complex, challenging, and politically contested space at times. We have to make sure we're getting the most high-quality information, connections, networks, and education, to deliver value to our Clients and the people we work with.

What do you want your legacy to be?

CHANTAL

I want my legacy to be about creating a world where people don't get judged on the colour of their skin. It's as simple as that. We've gotten so comfortable with looking at people and making up our own negative assumptions. This is what continues to create a disconnect for humanity.

I grew up thinking Aboriginal people were drunk, lazy criminals, because I didn't know the truth. And now, as the proud mother of an Aboriginal child, I don't want anyone to look at my baby and think like that! I want people to look at my children and think they're kind, intelligent, connected, beautiful little souls who have the ability to make a positive contribution to Australian society. This is the experience I get when I'm out with Aboriginal people in the community. We need to be led by our hearts in terms of connecting with other human beings, not misconceptions we have in our heads.

KIA

I agree. There's a postcard I bought a few years ago. It has a quote from Martin Luther King's I have a Dream speech, which reads *I have a dream that my four little children will one day live in a nation where they will not be judged by the color of their skin but by the content of their character.* I also look forward to the day when there isn't that division. When we aren't so free to label everyone.

I get that to make sense of the world people feel the need to belong, but at the end of the day we're all just human beings. We're all different interpretations of the experiences we have. It's not better or worse. Just different. I hope we can celebrate and appreciate what diversity brings. In Australia if we've come this far in two-hundred years since colonisation, maybe we'll soon have an Aboriginal or Torres Strait Islander prime minister. I hope that happens in our lifetime.

Do you have any other quotes you'd like to share?

KIA

When I played basketball, I had to memorise quotes. There are two that stick with me. One is by Gandhi. "You must be the change you wish to see in the world." It was my mum who told me that quote. We were travelling in to Kununurra when I was around sixteen, and she said, "You know, Kia, we don't see the world the way things are. We see the world the way we are." And I was like "Who said that?" She said, "Oh, this Indian bloke." Then she started telling me about Gandhi and about *The Celestine Prophecy*. That's kind of stuck with me.

The other quote that's quite beautiful is by Marianne Williamson. "It is our light, not our darkness, that most frightens us." Nelson Mandela read that speech in 1994 when he became president. I was about eleven years old. I wanted to make a difference and knew this was not how the story was going to end.

There's a quote that says when writing the story of your life to make sure you're the one holding the pen. For women, there are so many influences, pressures, and obligations. It comes down to standing in your own power and saying this is where I'm going to commit my focus, energy, and resources.

You say you want to change the narrative. You're two young women walking into major corporations. How do they perceive you? What are some of their reactions?

CHANTAL:

Your dream may not be everyone's cup of tea, and that's okay, but if you're the one holding the pen you can write your own story. Then you can turn around and look back on what you've done, particularly in the face of adversity.

CHAPTER 7: Kia Dowell and Chantal Harris

Kia and I walk into these big corporations, and the receptionist will sometimes ask if we're lost. We just say, "No, we're here to have a meeting with your CEO." They look at us like we're just these young women wandering around their lobby! I think that's the power of writing your own story. You build the resources that will allow you to have independence and do what you want to do. That takes a lot of hard work and effort, but what is the alternative? Settling for doing work you don't like for other people? That's hard and takes too much effort. We know why we're here. We know the value we can add, and we can change their perception of young women. That's what fuels us.

KIA

I do like that we're different, because it disrupts people's thinking.

So, you feel you offer a unique perspective as younger women?

KIA

When we started our business, we spent a lot of time up front getting clear on what we brought to the table as younger people. Market researchers will pay thousands of dollars to find out what Gen X and Y are after. The investment we've made in ourselves goes hand in hand with the value we bring. What we've found is that there's an intangible value men have placed on the perspective we bring, because it isn't what they're surrounded by in the boardroom. That's something businesses and key decision makers are starting to see. There's value in having that diversity of perspective. We get to be in that league.

What is your advice for women who want to start a business?

CHANTAL

For any woman wondering whether they should start a business, my advice is that now is the best time to do it. Look at all of the companies that have been able to build their wealth based on information other people didn't have. The internet blew that apart. Everyone has the information now. Actually, there's too much information. The three things that make businesses successful these days is to be able to create change, nurture relationships, and collaborate to bring combined resources to the table with that information, as opposed placing all of the importance on the information itself.

Women do that hands down better than men! We're in such a different space in the business world. In the next ten years, female entrepreneurship will create so much change. It's going to be exciting to see that, because the "old boys' club" mentality is going to be a thing of the past.

CHAPTER 7: Kia Dowell and Chantal Harris

THE CULTURAL CONNECTION CODE - WHO ARE WE?

The Cultural Connection Code is one of Australia's leading Aboriginal Consulting and Coaching Companies. We specialise in creating the cultural connection needed to accelerate business and leadership development in organisations and communities across Australia.

In 2012, Kia Dowell and Chantal Harris, co-founded **THE CULTURAL CONNECTION CODE,** a creative, collaborative, and intelligent for-profit consultancy specialising in bringing Australia's Aboriginal and non-Aboriginal people together to co-design innovative solutions to address business and social issues.

Our consulting, coaching, and training services have been infused with a carefully crafted CODE. It's made up of a unique combination of neuroscience and traditional Australian Aboriginal wisdom that accelerates business and leadership whenever corporate culture and Aboriginal culture merge together.

We believe we can achieve genuine social change through sustainable economic development when we work with people and communities to design their own futures and deliver social and economic independence. We can all contribute to positive social change in a way that respects cultural diversity alongside cultivating achievements through community and commercial endeavours.

What We Do Well

We are committed to leveraging opportunities created through technological, financial, social, political, and environmental changes to deliver benefits beyond their scope. It's the new way of doing business.

This innovative and unique way of delivering value for our clients creates a shift in organisational culture to reshape enterprises that are not only sustainable but also create positive social impacts through corporate contribution.

Our Philosophy

We are often asked what makes us different from other consulting companies, and the truth is that it's not necessarily what we do but how we do it. Our team of specialists have been hand-picked as highly skilled and trusted professionals in their respective fields of expertise and for their ongoing connection to country and culture.

Ninety percent of our team is made up of Aboriginal people who represent various Aboriginal groups across Western Australia. Our team is based in their own regions and connected to the aspirations of their own communities. You can feel safe in the knowledge that you will get results when you work with us, because we've spent decades testing and refining the code to get it right just for you, including being guided by our cultural protocols.

CHAPTER 7: Kia Dowell and Chantal Harris

What Clients Have Said:

We work beside Kia and Chantal as partners increasing the capacity of businesses. We are continuously impressed by their fresh approach, and more importantly, their deep level of understanding of Aboriginal culture and communities and how to build effective business models to achieve financial and social outcomes. It's a very valuable skill combination."

~ Aboriginal Partner Organisation

We really enjoyed working with Kia and Chantal on the Gelganyem Strategic Plan. We have not seen that genuine level of engagement combined with a good balance of knowledge about our communities and the business world before. We feel like we own our Strategic Plan and can talk to our Mob about it. It would be good if all consultants worked this way."

~ Member of the Gelganyem Strategic Plan Sub-Committee

Keeping You Updated

As a way to share all of this goodness with you and positively impact more Aboriginal Communities, we publish *Pathfinders*, a free, inspiring, value-packed digital magazine delivered straight to your inbox every month.

Simply go to our website and click on the **Pathfinders link** to sign up today.

*"To be yourself
in a world that is
constantly trying to
make you something
else is the greatest
accomplishment."*

Ralph Waldo Emerson

CHAPTER 8

Philippa Ross

CHAPTER EIGHT

Philippa Ross

Philippa is an Energy Health Consultant, Reiki practitioner, Energy dance and Equine-Assisted Learning facilitator, author, and freelance writer. She defines herself as an Enthusiologist and Personal Intelligence Philosopher. Her work is centred on energising and harmonising people and the planet. Using her family motto, '"Hope Lightens Difficulties', she helps people discover a sense of self and their True North, so they can use their value to add value to the world around them.

I connected with Philippa through the Inspirational Bible, *a book of 365 inspirational stories from around the world we both contributed to. I've never met her face to face, but we've had countless conversations via social media and Skype. I was intrigued by her pilgrimage to find her true self and her plans to pay homage to her Great, Great, Great Grandfather. This is a story of resilience and fortitude that turns failure on its head.*

Tell me about your early life

My story starts when I was eleven years old. My world changed from living in a close-knit suburban community to an isolated country lifestyle hundreds of miles away from everything and everyone I'd ever known.

My father, at the age thirty eight, decided he wanted to become a farmer, even though he'd never done anything like it before in his life. Uprooting his family and diving into the unknown was a particularly courageous leap for dad, who is a man known for his cautious, calculated approach to life. But leap he did, along with the support from my mum, who quite literally mucked in tending the land, animals, and us children.

They were fortunate to find a farm next door to my uncle, who was a great help to us all. We had a couple of hundred acres of arable land, some pigs, chickens, and a small herd of beef cows that mum named after all of her old friends. It was so

CHAPTER 8: Philippa Ross

much fun. A real team family affair that turned out to be some of the best years of my life and the source of invaluable inspiration in later years.

Mum had her own 'house cow', Diana, named after her new best friend. The cow provided the family with wholesome, full fat, unadulterated milk. Diana then had a calf, Emma, which meant we had more milk than we knew what to do with, so Mum took herself off on a course to learn the art of cheese making. Before we knew it, she'd turned the old granary into a cheese shop that stocked about seventy cheeses from around the world, plus our very own brand of soft and hard cheeses, butter, and yoghurt. I worked in the shop from the age of thirteen for a couple of years, making all of the produce, serving at the counter, and giving talks to visiting tourists.

I developed an appreciation for the quality of what I call 'real' food and how important the nutrients in the ground are for cultivating an environment where the seeds would grow and develop into healthy crops to feed the animals and us. How, in turn, what the animals ate affected the quality of the meat and milk they produced.

I was lucky enough to have my own horse. Kestrel was a twenty-seven year old mining pony who'd spent her entire life in the mines carrying coal to the surface. She was a nightmare to catch. I guess she thought I was going to send her back down the mines again. Once caught, she'd settle down. We had heaps of fun together. She had a lovely, trusting nature. Her back had a large dip, which made it impossible to put a saddle on her, so I used to ride her bare back. My friend, Tina, and I would disappear into the hills for the day with a picnic lunch. Kestrel had a foal that I called Pegasus, or Gus for short. He used to let me lie on his tummy out in the paddock, and together, we'd solve the world's problems. Then life got busy. I reached another stage of life where boys became more interesting, and the horses were sold.

Mum and Dad loved their lifestyle, but after six years the financial stress of a never-decreasing overdraft forced them to downsize to a small holding. We had just a few paddocks to keep the house cows so mum could establish another cheese shop, and Dad went out to work. Before long, the shift drove a wedge between them, and they went their separate ways.

How did that impact you?

It had a big impact on me. I was in my final year at school and failed all of my exams. I left home soon after; just wanting my independence and to be away from it all. Subconsciously I associated failure with money and relationships. Life's failures and faux pas provide invaluable lessons and great opportunities to explore different avenues to help you find your True North.

At about that time I was out driving with a friend, when I spotted Kestrel's distinctive back in a paddock, so I asked my friend to pull over. I wanted to see if it really was her. Upon calling her name, her ears pricked up, and she trotted over to me for the first time ever. It was an extraordinary experience that has stayed with me to this day and made all the more special as my name means 'lover of horses'. I had tears pouring down my cheeks as she nuzzled her head into me, like a thank you for the good times. It was a moment that connected me to the power of horses as mentors for our own development, something I'd revisit twenty five years later. But in that moment her response helped me to understand the obstacles we're subjected to are future lessons that help build resilience, confidence, and courage to accomplish what really matters to us, so we can live our lives in alignment with our true selves.

Was that the realisation that gave you the courage to pursue a degree in Psychology?

Subjectively, yes. I didn't actually set out to get a degree, which was probably a good thing at the time, or I'd never have attempted it. We've fast forwarded fifteen years here. I was at a point in my life where I'd consciously connected to something that really mattered to me: my children. I was searching for information on how I could understand and help ttheir development. I found the baby books too shallow. I wanted something more.

The Open University in England were offering study units in Child Development, so I enrolled. I discovered a new love of learning and a hidden ability to write. I passed the exam, which spurred me on to enrol in another year, after which I gained an Advanced Diploma in Child Development. I was inspired to take another unit the following year on education, as my eldest child was just about to start school. I passed again and realised I was halfway through a degree, so I decided to carry on. By that time, I'd created a real thirst for knowledge. This was fortunate, because in my fifth year I failed the exam. I'd achieved pass marks

CHAPTER 8: Philippa Ross

in all of the papers but had a complete meltdown in the exam room. I couldn't remember a thing! But I was determined to finish my degree the following year, so with the phenomenal support from the university, I embarked on my final year with two exams looming at the finishing post.

The University introduced me to the art of visualisation. I remember taking the dog for a walk every morning and visualising myself receiving my degree. It worked. There were obviously other strategies I had to put into place, like Post-it notes all over the house, but I knew I was capable, and just because I'd failed once didn't mean I'd do it again. My studies and the visualisation technique rewired my brain to overcome the belief system that had hardwired me to think I was a failure. I can still remember opening the results envelope and staring in disbelief. The girl who'd been classed as illiterate now had an Honours Degree in Psychology. The irony was spectacular. A person who'd failed English and Science at school had accomplished a degree that combined both subjects.

What did you wind up doing with your degree?

I secured a job with a leading Psychiatrist, Dr George Hibbert. He ran an assessment centre for parents who were in the court system to establish their parenting capabilities. A year later I emigrated to New Zealand with high praise from Dr Hibbert, who recommended I start my own centre. After a year of settling my family into a new country, I started my own counselling service, Cherish Wellbeing. I was told by the social services organisation, Child, Youth and Family (CYF), that I needed to have a master's degree before they'd consider using me. I was done with studying, so I thought I'd take my time to build a reputation for myself. After eight short months, CYF rang me to ask if I'd be an agent for them.

This must have given you a great opportunity to affect change.

Yes, but it was hard, as the majority of cases were for six-week periods only. It takes time to build trust with someone, especially when they're not open to being counselled. I remember one particular case where I got the chance to work with the client for nearly a year, and when we went to court the judge commended me for the great job I'd done. I accepted the compliment but pointed out that I had merely facilitated the change. The client had created the change herself. It was incredibly rewarding to see how a person could turn their life around with support from someone who believed in them.

It was during this time the seeds of my Personal Intelligence Programme (PIP) were planted. Those seeds have been cultivating for about eight years as I acquired wisdom from the knowledge and experience I've gained during that time. I reconnected to my love of horses through a friend, Ian, who ran a trekking business. He showed me how horses respond to human behaviour by mirroring our approach to life and the relationship we have with ourselves. His work was phenomenal. I wound up training to become an Equine Learning Facilitator. Not long after, I decided to create a two-day Total Wellbeing event featuring Ginette McDonald, an iconic New Zealand comedienne. She was to administer laughter as the best medicine in her role as Mistress of Ceremonies for twenty speakers who offered advice in a variety of different holistic, natural health modalities. I gained some lifelong friends and a wealth of information but lost $20,000 putting on the event. The shortfall amounted to more than just the money. It also had an impact on my marriage.

What happened?

The pressure leading up to and after the event was the straw that broke the camel's back for my marriage. Teenage children, early menopause, and a husband with a completely different idea of parenting to mine, along with his own childhood issues, all added fuel to the frustration of failing and losing so much money. I tried to piece things together, but over the next year the chasm between us grew bigger and bigger. I decided to end the marriage, as I could feel my physical, mental, emotional, and spiritual self being drained.

It seems both your professional and personal life were in turmoil. What did you do?

My work took a back seat. I focused my attention on supporting my children and helping them through the change. I wrestled with the guilt of breaking up my family. Over time I forgave myself for the disruption I'd caused, while also honouring my courage to put my own needs above everyone else's. It was a hard call for any woman, particularly when you have children. I used my time to study quantum physics and how our external world affects our internal being. The information helped me to nurture myself and develop my programme, using myself as a guinea pig. I wrote and published *Cherish*, a chick-lit novel, and then started writing a mind, body, soul book I've called *Life's a Load of Balls! How to Master the Game of Life*. It's a book that carries the acquisition of all of my

CHAPTER 8: Philippa Ross

learning and provides people with the tools to see their own value, so they can use it to add value to the world.

I enjoyed new pastimes, going to Ceroc dance lessons, and joining an art class doing pastel portraits. I found a delicious man who's become my rock. He makes me laugh, and most importantly, allows me to be me.

Three years ago, I received an email from Greenpeace that said the Ross Sea in Antarctica was being considered for marine protection. I did a double take. My Great, Great, Great Grandfather, Sir James Clark Ross, was the man responsible for discovering the Ross Sea in 1841. I phoned my father in England to see if he knew anything, but he didn't, so I phoned Greenpeace, introduced myself, and told them about my heritage. They told me about a new documentary due to be premiered in Auckland the following month that focused on the Ross Sea called *The Last Ocean*. I contacted the film director, a New Zealand man named Peter Young of Fisheye Films, who invited me to the first screening at the New Zealand Film Festival.

My daughter came with me. She held my hand as I wept throughout the film. I was mesmerised and deeply touched by the scenes and the devotion of the team that had dedicated seven years of their lives to raising awareness about the Ross Sea. It's deemed to be the last intact eco marine system left in the world. Although I'd known about my ancestor's polar expeditions, I'd never considered the significance of my lineage until this point in my life.

Needless to say, I've become actively involved ever since. I was asked to speak at the Commission for the Conservation of Antarctic Marine Living Resources (CCAMLR) meeting in 2012 in the hope my heritage would sway representatives from the twenty-four countries to grant marine protection to the Ross Sea, as its value was also about preserving our legacy and the health of all future generations. All four meetings to date have been unsuccessful, but I'm hopeful that by the end of October 2015, it will finally receive the protection it so deserves. It would be so fitting. January 2016 marks the 175th anniversary since James' remarkable find.

How has this experience set you on a new course?

It's not a new course. It's more one that adds meaning and depth to the course I'm already on. Connecting to my heritage created an *a-ha* moment for me when

I realised James used the earth's magnetic field to chart his course across the ocean. He first discovered the North magnetic pole in 1831, and then ventured south in an attempt to find the South Pole. I use the earth's magnetic field to help people chart a course to find their True North.

My role has evolved to help people understand how the earth's magnetic field affects their health and what they can do to create changes that will have a positive impact for themselves and the planet. We know everything is energy. I liken humans to balls of energy, hence the name of my book. Each and every one of us vibrates at a different frequency that continuously changes according to our surroundings. If the environment we're in resonates with us, we're levered to a higher frequency, and our energy increases. If our surroundings don't resonate, our energy decreases, and we become disconnected from ourselves and the world around us. Continual dissonance causes what I call the *D syndrome*. Disillusion, distress, depression, and disease.

My mission is to educate and raise awareness about the importance of valuing the diversity of human nature and helping people connect, direct, and transform their energy into areas that matter to them. I believe this will have an exponential effect on the planet by allowing both to flourish.

How does your programme help achieve your mission?

PIP helps people get to know the spiritual, emotional, mental, and physical parts of themselves. It helps them understand what matters to them and how they can increase their energy, which ultimately increases their potential. It allows them to establish their roots and build a strong foundation that gives them a sense of self worth, so they feel they can make a valuable contribution to the world.

The entire programme uses language to help people relate to and remember the learning, along with colour and cartoons to solidify and add meaning. It begins with an insight into the senses, as they're key to building a strong connection to our environment. The spiritual element of the programme is about identifying your qualities and what matters to you. The V.A.L.U.E technique allows you create a set of personal guidelines to build trust and confidence in yourself. The C.H.E.R.I.S.H goal setting tasks give you the opportunity to align seven different areas of life with the seven energy centres that govern the health of the body. It ensures you're dispersing your energy into all of the areas for balanced

CHAPTER 8: Philippa Ross

fulfilment. The exercise helps to exorcise any subconscious conditioning, so you create solutions as you go. The S.M.A.R.T.E.R technique enables you to break down your goals to create a measure of your own success. The emotional element of the programme addresses what I call the *F Factors*. The feelings created by energy in motion and how to manage discord. The mental aspect of the programme enables you to create a H.E.A.D.S.P.A.C.E to rewire the neural paths to overcome 'can't', 'should' and 'need to' beliefs that keep you stuck behind the eight ball. The physical element provides ways to establish healthy eating, sleeping, and moving habits to sustain your strength.

How did it come about?

It evolved, just like my degree. I didn't set out to create my book or the programme. They're an accumulation of my personal experiences, professional qualifications, and insights I gained from my children, family, friends and clients that will make a difference to a raft of societal problems, especially depression and suicide. I wanted to create something that would impact people's ability to have the courage of their convictions and confidence to grab life by the balls. Something that would help them create a life where they felt healthy, hopeful, and whole without having to endure years of compromising their true self to please everyone but themselves. Life is definitely a whole lot easier when you know yourself and trust your intuition.

What keeps you inspired, and what is your ultimate goal for your program?

My children, Dominic and Toni, are the source of my inspiration. I wouldn't be half the person I am today without them. They keep me grounded and are not afraid to question the validity of what I say and do.

My ultimate aim is for PIP to become a part of teacher training and an integral part of the school curriculum to help children grow up with a sense of self and belonging with the freedom to explore what matters to them. My motivation is fuelled by a desire to create a change in our education system. I had firsthand experience of how the system stifled my potential, as well as that of my children and many clients, leaving us all questioning our ability to be of value and fit in with the world. I want the diversity of human nature to be respected and children given the opportunity to grow and develop naturally with the support they need to explore their curiosity.

We are not commodities. People matter. Our environments would flourish if we valued social capital above the current mighty dollar.

What is your advice for those who feel guilty taking time for themselves?

You must invest in yourself. One of the mistakes women, particularly mothers, make is to tend to everybody else's needs before their own. It's important to care for yourself first. Your energy affects the energy of the people around you. If you're energised, it will lift everyone else. Our roles have changed considerably in the past century. Gone are the days where women are expected to stay at home with the children. Some women choose to, while others have to work. Some run a business from home. Whatever your decision, choose it because it's what you want, as opposed to doing it because it's what others expect of you.

It's important to sustain your identity beyond being a mum. Many women feel lost when the children leave home, because they've invested so much time and energy into their children, they lose the connection to their own identity and associate their role with who they are. Mothers need to look after all aspects of themselves and tend to their own needs first while taking the time to energise themselves, so they're spiritually, emotionally, mentally and physically strong enough to support their families.

It's important you treat yourself in the same way you'd treat your best friend. Take a bath with candles. Ask somebody else to look after the children for at least an hour a week. Take turns with a group of people, so you have that time to yourself. Step into nature whenever you can. Walk in the sunshine, and breathe deeply.

Slow conscious breathing is the best way to manage stress. Breathe in slowly to the count of eight, so you feel it filling up your diaphragm. Hold for eight, and breathe out for sixteen. If you can only do three or four at first, that's fine. This simple exercise recalibrates your entire body, because the adrenal glands are unable to produce the stress hormone when they're so well oxygenated. The more you do it, the calmer you'll be.

CHAPTER 8: Philippa Ross

What's your next adventure?

Thanks to the generosity of Heritage Expeditions CEO, Rodney Russ, I'm going on a thirty-five day cruise to the Antarctic in February to celebrate the 175th anniversary since James discovered the Antarctic continent. I'm currently working on a project to get 175 prominent individuals and organisations who value the Ross Sea, the Antarctic, and/or the environment to write a letter that will become part of a book to honour the occasion. No doubt, I'll end up writing a book about this special pilgrim voyage, too. I've already been invited to Bali to talk at a women's conference, which I'm doing after I've completed a business mentoring scholarship I won from entering the iLab Global Impact Awards.

I've just terminated my full-time job with the Northern Advocate and am about to relaunch my business. I'm going from Cherish Wellbeing to Philippa Ross, Enthusiologist & Personal Intelligence Philosopher. I'm putting my best step forward to gain credibility and traction from books and articles I've written and contributed to. I'm going to finally finish writing *Life's a Load of Balls*, so I can use the book to create momentum in my business. One day I hope to establish my own school, an intergenerational learning pod where young and old share their wisdom.

What advice would you give to people who've lost their self confidence?

Take a deep breath and remember you're unique and invaluable. Aristotle said, "Knowing yourself is the beginning of all wisdom." Take the time to connect to your own wisdom. Invest in PIP for yourself. Life is a precious gift. Don't waste your energy trying to please everyone else. Invest your time, energy, and finances into what matters to you. Unwrap the gift inside you and use it to light up the world. Acknowledge the smallest of steps you take, as they'll bring you closer to where you want to be. Keep your eye on the ball. Energy flows where your attention goes.

How can people find you?

People can find me on my website, www.Philippaross.com or my Facebook page – Philippa Ross – PIP – Enthusiologist. Enthusiologist on LinkedIn and Twitter, Philippa Ross on Google+, and Cherishyoursoul on Skype.

"Nothing great was ever achieved without enthusiasm."

~Ralph Waldo Emerson

Philippa Ross has carved a unique niche for herself as an Enthusiologist and Personal Intelligence Philosopher. She uses her playful, down-to-earth nature to cultivate and sustain an environment for growth and development for people and the planet, the way nature intended.

CHAPTER 8: Philippa Ross

Philippa has combined her personal experiences, professional qualifications in psychology, and passion for the environment into a skill-set she calls the Personal Intelligence Programme (P.I.P) to help you find your True North.

The programme focuses on the spiritual, emotional, mental, and physical parts of being human, to give you the tools to master the game of life. Enhancing your wellbeing will enable you to create a measure of your own success and accomplishments, build the confidence and courage to be true to yourself, and grab life by the balls, so you have a bloody good time while you have the privilege of living.

Master the Game of Life – Connect. Pause. Engage. Respond
- **Connect** to what inspires you – the true nature of who you are. (spiritual)
- **Pause** to develop awareness and understanding of what your emotions (energy in motion) are telling you. (emotional)
- **Engage** your brain to consciously attend to matter that matters to you. (mental)
- **Respond** with actions that harmonise your soul, heart, mind, and body matter to work as a team. (physical)

Like Aristotle, Philippa believes knowing yourself is the beginning of all wisdom. P.I.P will help you connect, direct, and transform your wisdom to reveal the depth of your own intelligence and what matters to you, so you can use your own value to add value to the world around you.

Philippa has an Honours Degree in Psychology, an Advanced Diploma in Child Development, is a Reiki practitioner, and an Equine-Assisted Learning and Energy Dance Facilitator. She's studied and researched quantum physics, positive psychology, human ecology, energy psychology, ontology, philosophy, epigenetics, and psychoneuroimmunology, in her quest to quench an insatiable thirst for knowledge and understanding about the intrinsically interconnected web of life and our connection to nature.

She's the Great, Great, Great Granddaughter of the Polar Explorer Sir James Clark Ross who charted the oceans to both Polar Regions using the earth's magnetic field to navigate his way. He discovered the North Magnetic Pole in 1831, and the Ross Sea and Ross Ice Shelf, Antarctica in 1841 while on a quest to find the South Pole.

We are all descendants of the ocean. It is the source of all life. It's crucial we protect our environment, as we're all part of a whole eco system that sustains the cycle of life. Our health, our internal eco system, is affected by the environment around us. Our ability to flourish is reliant on our capacity to connect to the universal intelligence and create an environment that harmonises humanity and the planet, the playground where we live out our lives

If we are full of enthusiasm for life, then the unknown reveals itself, and our universe changes directions

~Paulo Coelho

CHAPTER 9

Suzanne Waldron

"It always seems impossible until it's done."

Nelson Mandela

CHAPTER NINE
Suzanne Waldron

Suzanne works with leaders and go-getters in her field of behavioural change. She has an unwavering vision that supports others to shift their thinking to doing. Working with people who have a powerful want for the world is what motivates her the most.

I first met Suzanne at the Pan Pacific Hotel in Perth when I was doing interviews for this book. She's a vibrant and happy person. You would never know the massive challenges she's gone through in her life. From the moment I met her, I felt like we'd already been friends for a long time. She has an important message that everyone should hear.

Tell me about your early life.

I'm from Kent, England. In my early years, my parents were both truck drivers, so I lived and travelled in Europe until about the age of five. Through a series of circumstances, when I was about eight years old my life turned upside down. Before I really knew the ways of the world, I had to adapt to a new and shocking way of life. My parents separated, and I went into foster care. It's difficult to lose your entire family and be put into the home of strangers, no matter how loving they may be.

My dad was having an affair with a teenager. It broke our family apart. My mum carried on driving trucks. She was very much a tomboy. She was also a manipulative person, as well as insecure, and consequently she got into dangerous relationships. While in foster care as a child, I would visit her. Nobody knew this, but her partner would treat me terribly. He once dragged me along the road until my feet bled. My mom would also shut me in my room and not speak to me.

I was just eight and so confused living in someone else's house, even though they were beautiful Dutch people who looked after me. It took its toll on me. One day I walked into the television room at school, and my legs gave way.

My neurology had just stopped working. The doctor told me I'd had a nervous breakdown. The stress caused my limbs to malfunction. After a court case, my dad got sole custody of me, and from then on I lived with him, his mistress, and my grandmother in their two-bedroom home in England.

It sounds like you were at a fragile point in your life, both emotionally and physically. Did moving in with your dad provide you a stable environment?

I did start to get into a normal life. It was good for a while, until I felt uncomfortable. I couldn't remain in the house. My dad was a strict and petty person early in my life. If I was living with him, and I cleaned my room, he would come through and put his finger along a windowsill. If he found dust there, he would turn that room upside down. He was so emotionally fragile himself. He was also consumed with his new wife, the mistress, who was eighteen by now. It was as if I was only needed for chores.

At fifteen, I eventually left my dad's and moved in with my mum. I was even planning on going to college, but it was just too difficult to be around her. She was manipulative and often lied. After a couple of months, I'd had enough of my mum trying to use me as a pawn in her world. She was just trying to leverage me most of the time for her own good. I craved love and attention. In desperation, I went to visit my boyfriend at his new place two hours away and didn't go back. That's how I became homeless at the age of fifteen.

You had gotten yourself out of a toxic situation, but that's a young age to be on your own. What happened?

My boyfriend was in staff quarters, and the people he was living with were old and had different old-world values. They didn't think it was appropriate for me to stay in his room. That meant I ended up living in fields or his car. It was rough, but it was one of the best decisions I've ever made. I wouldn't change it for the world. It gave me independence and freedom. I was manipulated a lot as a young person, pulled from pillar to post emotionally and often used as a pawn.

Did you ever get back in touch with your parents?

There were a lot of times I wanted to end the relationship with my mum, but I didn't want to hurt her. I didn't know if either of us could cope with that. We'd had quite a good relationship over Skype for some time in my twenties, but when

CHAPTER 9: Suzanne Waldron

I went to visit her a few years ago she was quite hurtful. I wanted to connect with her and be a real mother and daughter. Amongst other spiteful things she said, she told me she felt hate when she looked at me, because I looked like my father, and she could never be a mother to me.

I thought about my visit with my mum for a good month afterwards. I kept thinking I was worth more than being slapped around the face metaphorically. I was allowing her to do it by being connected to her, so I decided to completely cut off the relationship. I believe it was a mutual agreement. This was empowering but also disappointing and sad. The connection between a mother and daughter is so important for a young girl. At the time of my visit with her, I also spent time with my dad. He died of a heart attack six months later. I'm pleased I followed my instincts and spent time with him. Even after his poor actions early in my life, he had tried to make it up in the last ten years of our relationship. I respected that and exercised forgiveness.

How did these experiences affect your other relationships?

For many years, even through my mid-to-late twenties, I was confused, angry, and hurt, and I acted that way. In all of my relationships, if anyone did anything wrong, I would dismiss them with no second chances. It came to a crux, and I realised I didn't want to feel that way anymore. It was tiring. That's when I decided I could change how I felt and acted. I started to learn more about human behaviour and figure out how I wanted to be in the world. It wasn't like this one critical moment of epiphany. It was an accumulation of watching people and using them as role models.

I relied on the kindness of strangers as I studied and worked on myself bit by bit, year by year, moment by moment. Then there came a point where I not only realised I was okay but that I could help others. My husband, who I've been with for nearly twenty years, has been a major inspiration and reason to be more loyal, caring, and persistent in relationships.

Who are some of your role models?

I've had some great role models. Since I was young, I've had a best friend whose name is also Suzanne. Her mum, Carol, told me a few years ago that my mum used to drop me off for play dates and leave me there for days. My mum didn't know it at the time, but this was the kindest thing she could have done for me.

I was so grateful. It's like the universe set my world right by bringing me Carol at an early age. I didn't have any other family. My grandmother died when I was eleven, on my birthday. Many others have been surrogate parents or pseudo family members as I moved through my life. I believe they have all led the way for me to truly flourish.

How were you able to incorporate these experiences into your work?

I believe it's important to get in touch with people's belief systems, values, and identity. How they use their senses to process and filter information in order to create their own stories. I work with people in many different formats to get them to shift their thinking as quickly as possible, because we all get hung up on our stories. I could have easily hung on to all of that stuff from my past and become a victim, thinking the world owed me. I could have thought I wasn't good enough, or I wasn't going to extend myself, because I'd been treated so badly or gone through life mistrusting others and myself.

I don't want people to get to the end of their life and feel it wasn't worth living. We don't have a lot of time on this earth, and nobody should live with regrets. I want people to be happy with the impression they've left on this world. I now speak internationally and work one-on-one to deeply help people. I have a master's degree in coaching and neuro-linguistics. I work with people and leaders in organisations intimately and quickly to shift their neurology, so they can interrupt their thought patterns and redirect them. It's like making new pathways in their head.

What inspires you?

My inspiration to pass on my knowledge comes from being extended so much kindness throughout my life. For instance, when I was fifteen and looking for a room to rent, the lady at the local pub let me use her telephone to receive messages, since nobody would give me a job if I didn't have a phone number or an address.

My first week's pay was £50, and the room I wanted to rent was £50 for a week. I went to the landlady with the note in my hand and told her it was all I had. She brought me in and said I could have two weeks plus food. Whereas I thought I was so mature, because I knew everything, she saw a fifteen year old standing on her doorstep with a £50 note and a bag of clothes.

CHAPTER 9: Suzanne Waldron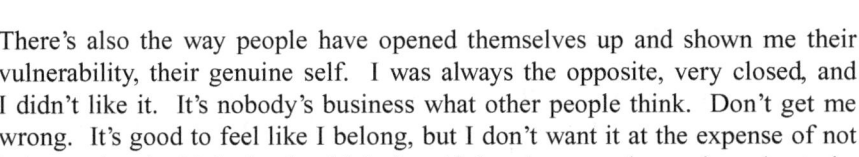

There's also the way people have opened themselves up and shown me their vulnerability, their genuine self. I was always the opposite, very closed, and I didn't like it. It's nobody's business what other people think. Don't get me wrong. It's good to feel like I belong, but I don't want it at the expense of not being authentic. Nobody should feel as if they have to change in order to be accepted.

What has being a woman in business taught you?

Being a woman in business, I've learned a lot. I think people have different gender energies. There are men with female energy, as well as those with male energy. Women can also have female or male energy. Quite honestly, I don't think as a woman I've had any different experiences than if I was a man. I have quite a lot of male energy as a woman. I've looked after myself since I was thirteen, including financially, so I'm forthright but with diplomacy and love.

Thousands of years of social history has seen the man play a certain role of business authority, and I agree that it's time to bring an equality to the genders in this modern age. I'm concerned that the movement of women coming into power can at times be at the expense of excluding men. I'd like to see a growing co-creation of this new age. The men in our lives are not the men of the past thousands of years. We need to remember to treat men like we want to be treated. Increasing self-worth and understanding your purpose, no matter what gender you are, is crucial. The underpinning key to being able to exist in business together. I'd like to continue to focus on that principal and not favour or exclude any one gender.

What is your message?

My message would be that there's no need to waste your life. You control your own thinking, your own emotions. In everything you do, you're unconsciously programming yourself. Through your habits and neurology, you can create anything you can conceive. It's about increasing self-belief and understanding. You have a choice in every circumstance. Even if both choices aren't that great, it's important to make the best of it and not dwell on your decision after it's been made. It's also crucial to find happiness in the little things and exercise kindness to ourselves and to others. You have control over who you are and how you want to be.

How would you like to change the world?

I believe it's not about removing problems. We all need to experience polarity. It's about minimising the negative impacts. We have bad times to appreciate the good times. What I would like to change is the way people hang on to their problems. Everyone needs to understand how to control their emotions and change their state of mind. To understand how they get triggered. I'm doing that now in my business, and I want to go a step further. The profits from my business go towards building a foundation for people between the ages of sixteen and twenty five. It's inspired by The School of Life with Alain De Botton. People in different countries would run it to expand it beyond me.

What have you learned about completing your goals?

When I was studying for my master's, I researched the topic of inner fulfilment and if we achieve it when we go beyond ourselves. Of course, the answer is yes. I interviewed Dr Fiona Wood, a plastic surgeon. She invented spray-on skin for burn victims that reduces the amount of time needed to produce enough cells to cover major burns. I also talked to Rabia Siddique, a criminal and human rights lawyer who in 2005 was sent to Basra to negotiate with captors at al-Jamiat Prison, only to nearly get beheaded and denied recognition for her bravery. She fought for justice and won. In speaking to this brave mix of people, both men and women, I developed an understanding of the process they went through to get from intention to completion, because there are so many people who have good intentions but never take action.

In total, I talked to six people who had accomplished something extraordinary. Every single person had exactly the same order of events. I studied their model of excellence, and the conclusion I drew was that it starts with self-efficacy. It means having strength of character and understanding who you are and what you believe in. Then it moves on to being empathic, which means being able to put yourself in someone else's shoes. It's also about selflessness. Caring about society as a whole and not just our own needs. And lastly, all of these people were in charge of their own fate. They made a choice about what they wanted to do and took action. It all leads back to strength of character. I called it the Pro-Social Model of Excellence. I have a free video series training program that includes steps people can take to improve their lives. It's on my website, suzannewaldron.com. I'd like for people to shift their thinking, and that's what I work on the most.

CHAPTER 9: Suzanne Waldron

What message do you have for people who are stuck and feel they can't achieve their goals?

People seem to think they need to know everything before they start a project. I've had some of the best successes in saying yes to people and having no idea where it would go. And if it didn't work out, I learned from that as well. I would like to see people do more than think about what they want. It's the inner voice that counts. Positive affirmations don't work if you don't believe them. The first step is believing in yourself. It's easy to say just do it, but if you have a little voice inside your head that doesn't believe it and says you're not worth it, then it will never work. I'd like to have people start with increasing their own trust within themselves. The rest will follow.

Every day make sure you follow through on your intention, no matter how small. And if you do, you need to remember to thank yourself. By doing this, your system, your neurology, changes. Those happy chemicals come, and your body will crave more of it. And as you start to increase trust within yourself, your belief will come.

Human Behavioural Specialist Suzanne Waldron

Suzanne's ability to work with people quickly and at a deep level sets her apart in her field of behavioural change. She provokes critical and generative thinking that impacts her clients and causes long-lasting inner change.

An intense passion drives Suzanne. She holds a strong belief that everyone should live fully and to their own standards. Many individuals and organisations have an emotional lack of awareness or self-limiting thinking that doesn't serve them and wastes their precious time while inhibiting results.

Suzanne feels it's the life lessons she's learned along the way, more than her degrees and accreditations, that really qualify her to do the work she does. As a child, she lived with a foster family and became homeless at age fifteen. It's these experiences and lessons that inspired Suzanne to find the peace, happiness, and success she enjoys today.

Suzanne is the published author of *A Flourishing Mind*, a book about her uplifting and powerful story that includes poignant lessons and messages and brings real change to those who read it. The book is endorsed by Penni Pike, Sir Richard Branson's PA of thirty-two years, and Rabia Siddique, humanitarian and human rights lawyer.

Suzanne's research through her own Master's Degree in Coaching enabled her to find a model of excellence that depicts how influential people really can lead beyond themselves and uncovers psychological determinates to support this type of leadership.

CHAPTER 9: Suzanne Waldron

Suzanne spent many years working in organisational development and change, as well as facilitation and coaching. She has a vast understanding for the humanistic business world she works within and now spends her days coaching, speaking, and writing all around the world. Suzanne has delivered her talks in Australia, Fiji, and New Zealand and is currently emerging in the U.S.

Suzanne is an ambassador for the organization R U OK? and spreads the message of meaningful conversations in order to save lives. She's also a director on a board for Uniting for Homelessness, which seeks to reduce Perth city homelessness by more than fifty percent and move people into employment.

Suzanne's qualifications:

- Master's Degree in Applied Coaching (Behavioural Change)
- Internationally Accredited ICF Coach
- Internationally Accredited Master NLP Practitioner (Neuro-Linguistic Programming)
- Certified Supervisor Coaching and NLP
- Extensive facilitation/speaking training through Fran Berry, including large-audience management and adult-based learning.

"See perfection in the imperfection. Life is a work of art. If we are not perfect why do we expect so much of others?"

Gaye O'Brien

CHAPTER 10

Fauza Beltz

CHAPTER TEN

Fauza Beltz

Fauza Beltz is a freelance interior designer and the owner and founder of BIF accessories. She believes it's not who you wear but what you wear. Her greatest passion is finding ways to live a life with intention and inspiring others to do the same.

Fauza is my sister in-law. We both married into the Beltz family. I had heard of her way before I met her. Even though this book mainly focuses on women in Australia, I needed to share her story. To me, Fauza embodies courage and resilience, love and success. Despite having a rough life, she has grown into a loving woman running an international business. She is one young lady to look out for.

Tell me about your early life.

I was born out of wedlock. My parents hadn't planned for me. As a result, my dad had no desire to live with my mother, and my mum wanted to get on with her life. I grew up in different homes. First I was raised by my maternal grandmother in the village of Kwale (Mombasa) in Kenya. I'll always be grateful to her, but it was a tough childhood.

When I was five, my paternal grandmother took me in, and I started a new life with her as my mum. But even here, I received no love. She always beat me. Even though I had expected love from her as the only person I lived with, that was not in the picture, so I had to fight for myself.

By the age of seven I could cook and wash my own clothes. I became mature, because I had to. I felt out of place when I saw families together, but then I just had to make up my mind to get good and used to it. What I missed most in my childhood was the love. There was no moment in my childhood when I would say I had a family that loved me.

CHAPTER 10: Fauza Beltz

I was in a day school that was two hours away on foot. I used to leave the house at six a.m. and return by about five thirty. When I got back home, most of the time there was no lunch. I'd go get the *ugali* (maize flour cooked with water to a porridge) or maybe there was *cassava* or yams. Whatever was there, I'd help myself to it. I decided early on not to whine about it all of the time, because it did me no good.

When I finished primary school, my father took me to a boarding school close to Nairobi. It was there a new chapter began for me. I met people detached from their parents and started to create some friendships. I only went home during holidays, although the word *home* might not be accurate, in the way most people consider it. I had to stay with my stepmother, who also didn't treat me as family. She always reminded me I was just a stepdaughter and therefore inferior to her own daughters. The only persons who welcomed me were the neighbours. One of them, Bernice, is still one of my best friends.

After boarding school, I studied at college and stayed with a cousin in Nairobi, as I no longer felt welcome in my stepmother's house. Because of this, I again had to walk two hours back and forth to school. After college, I started my working life as a waitress. I didn't have any money to buy a uniform, but Bernice helped me. In my second job as a hotel hostess, I met my husband who showed an interest in me and didn't seem to care where I came from. A year into our relationship, I got pregnant. We married, and I decided that when I became a mother, everything would be different for my child, who would grow up with love.

How did becoming a wife and mother change you?

My husband and son gave me a new life. They gave me confidence to accept me for who I am. A woman people listen to. Motherhood has given me this zeal. I will always be there for my son in good and bad times. I have an open mind and tell myself it doesn't matter sometimes what's right, and my past has nothing to do with the present. I am in charge. I am responsible for my life and the life of my child.

I guess this confidence came about after I realized how much power I had within me. It's up to me to decide what I want to do with my life. I spend a lot of time with my son, Jasper, and I try to teach him as much as I can about self worth and how to be a loving person. I never want him to feel the way I did as a child. I love him dearly.

My husband is my best friend and my first mentor. He's a good listener and always gives his own opinion in an open, positive way that encourages me. I came to realize it doesn't matter what everyone thinks of you. In the end it's about who you believe you are. So if my family and I are all on the same page, it takes a blink of an eye to make a decision. It's that easy.

What message do you want to send by telling your story?

I think it's important to tell my story if I can help someone who is where I used to be and thinks they can't do anything about it. When I look at my young self, I see a girl who was naive, insecure, and hopeless. The world looked black to her. But once I opened up and talked to people, I started to gain confidence. I realised I wasn't the only one. Sometimes when we have a problem, we hold onto it and think it's the biggest problem in the world, and there's no way out.

What we all need to do is go out there and help someone who has an even bigger problem. It gets us out of feeling sorry for ourselves, and we can feel good in the process. I think it's important to be honest and let people know we need help. I've learnt if you don't ask, nobody will know what you really want or what you're going through. The reason I didn't tell anyone for a long time is because I was afraid of being judged. That was my biggest problem. It was only when I received love and had many talks with my husband that I realised my fear was created by myself and not by the environment. He taught me to convince myself it really doesn't matter.

For example, I participate in some workshops in Dubai. These conferences are focussed on business development, and it's a great platform for networking and learning new skills for my business. When I got to the conference room, it felt like thirty well-dressed women were staring at me. I'm always a smart, casual mum who dresses for the occasion, but nowadays I don't mind how people look at me.

What I'm learning is to have an open mind. If someone or something comes into your life and it will help, grab it. Otherwise just let it fly away. It takes a lot of courage to let go, but once you start loving and approving of yourself, everything falls into place. There's no greater love than the love you give to yourself.

CHAPTER 10: Fauza Beltz

I hope my story will help someone who has given up hope. I want to tell let them know they are not who people say they are. They have so much power. I wouldn't want people to feel sorry for me. That's not my intention. I want them to know that sometimes situations are not what they seem. If we accept who we are, we can create peace within ourselves.

Most of the time people feel bad because of self-doubt or lack of confidence. I mean, we all have that sometimes, but what's important is if you have an idea, don't just sit back. Get up and do it. It's not a problem to ask sometimes how to go about it. But be careful who you go to. There are people who will discourage you. So who is the right person? Your social network matters. Make sure you surround yourself with people who encourage and inspire you. If you don't try, you'll never know. We all have to start from somewhere.

What inspires you?

Passion inspires me. We moved to Dubai in 2011 because of my husband's new job. The city is full of energy, day and night, and it tells you to get up and do something. There are inspirations everywhere, so it's the creativity, the country, the expat life of it. I do what I do, because I love it. I never feel tired when I have a client coming over. I always tell myself I can juggle it all. To work on what's important and find balance. Then everything else will fall into place. If you find that balance, you can do what you never thought yourself capable of.

Tell me about your company, BIF.

I started Beltz Inspirations by Fauza (BIF) almost a year ago as a blog to share my ideas on décor fashion, and then I thought of starting my own jewellery collection. It's been almost a year now, and the collection is doing well so far. I always have a new collection, and it's inspired by the Maasai of Kenya. I believe every woman needs something unique and intimate. I design and choose all of the pieces, and then I figure out how to mix the style and colour pallets. The mixing is done by woman in Kenya. It feels good to support them financially. That was one of the reasons I started BIF accessories. To do something for society in Kenya.

I'm also obsessed with posting it on social media. I feel a little guilty, because I'm just learning fashion, and I want to tell these women they don't have to struggle with it. It's not that difficult, because I believe it's not who you wear but what you wear. I always tell my clients it's important to dress for your body type. I don't want to brag, but if you put the simplest items together with a BIF necklace, you will look amazing.

You also have an interior design business.

I call it more of a hobby. When we moved to Dubai, we were in this beautiful, big, empty, and echo-filled villa. That's when the passion started. I didn't want to just buy items and put them together, because I'd be creating a showroom rather than a home. I started taking design workshops before I moved to short courses. Then I went back to school to get a diploma in Interior Design. I already have clients. I get people who ask for my advice, but I'm just freelancing. My key message is that you don't have to work hard or spend a lot of money to have a beautiful home. It's the simple things that make the difference.

Do you have any quotes you'd like to share?

I do have some favourite quotes. One is by Oprah Winfrey. She says, "If you don't know what your passion is, realize that one reason for your existence on earth is to find it." Then there's one I'm obsessed with by Bill Rancic. He always says you don't have to be the smartest person in the world. All you need to do is work hard and believe in what you're doing. Another one is by Louise Hay. She says, "Don't be afraid to be you. The world needs your unique brand of awesomeness."

CHAPTER 10: Fauza Beltz

BIF Design

BIF Design focuses on providing interior design consulting with specific proposals for furniture, art pieces, decorator fabric, and accessories for the home and office that complements the design theme.

What you get with BIF Design:

- Furniture, accessories, and art pieces through special purchase arrangements with local shops or local craftsman.

- A unique client experience from a professional interior designer qualified and capable of meeting the needs of demanding clients with high expectations.

- Access to a wide and unique selection of new and antique furniture, accessories, and special-order decorator fabrics.

*"The caged bird
sings because
it has a song."*

CHAPTER 11

Fur Wale

CHAPTER ELEVEN

Fur Wale

Fur is the owner of SHE Talks®, a customised speaker training platform that enables entrepreneurial women, and women who are small business owners, to participate in an online mentor-led training.

The first time I met Fur was at the Foundation for Young Australians offices. She was kind and soft spoken. As we talked about love, life, and social change, I could see the passion in her eyes. She wants to make a difference in people's lives. She inspired me and made me want to know more about this woman and the impact she is making. Her story is quite confronting, but we can all relate. It's raw, and she does not sugar coat. I think the more we talk about the actual issues, the closer we get to solving them.

WARNING: Sensitive topics regarding sexual abuse and suicide.

Do you have anything to share before we get started?

I share my story in honour of those who helped to sculpt me into who I am today. The way I speak my truth, the way I am in the world. As traumatic as these stories are, there is a sense of surety I now possess, that I would not trade. For it is in the journey from child to adult that we seek and (hopefully) claim our personal truths. I share these stories and my insights as a gift to uplift those who seek to find theirs.

Tell me about your early life. What were you like as a young girl?

I grew up proud of my parents, because they gave me the kind of childhood they couldn't have. As they both came from religious families, they weren't able to truly express themselves. At least, not the way they craved to.

It was quite different for my two younger brothers and me. We were rarely told how to behave. We talked matters through as a family. All of the potential consequences were explained to us, and we were provided the opportunity to give

CHAPTER 11: Fur Wale

our perspective. My parents gave us choices and encouraged each of us to follow through with our decisions. As a result, we gained a sense of responsibility.

My parents actively sought to understand each of us as individuals, in order to best place great trust in us. They allowed us to be ourselves: adventurous, explorative, and creative. We were close, loving, affectionate and supportive. My family were my best friends. As I look back, I can see my parents demonstrated courage and adaptability, as this liberal way of raising children brought with it a lot of uncertainty for them. Because they allowed us to be independent thinkers, I became switched on. Thankfully, my parents fostered an environment of openness and honesty, and for this reason I never felt the need to lie. I always felt I could be authentically me. I accept this great gift as my foundation in life.

I started out as a soft-spoken girl who was shy, at least until I got to know you. Then you would become my audience to whom I would excitedly expound upon my favourite topics, which consisted of what I was curious about or had read about. My interests were quite broad. I was not content with being told what to do, yet I would do anything I could for someone if they asked for my help. It felt natural for me to be generously loving and kind to everyone.

I had an independent streak that set me off on many solo adventures as a young person, such as boldly undertaking a journey from home to take a train to an unknown destination, not knowing how to go back. I'm thankful the police kindly took me home on that occasion. Another adventure sent my dad into a spin, but it was worth it. I 'ran away from home' overnight, just to see what it was like.

I managed my first, second, and third businesses successfully from my cubby house before the age of ten. Later, I worked a big paper round. I offered my services to the neighbourhood to do odd jobs, so I could make big purchases, such as the hundred-dollar strobe light kit I wanted to build for my sleep out. Often I would sneak out of school to drape myself along the branch of my favourite gumtree and dream up many other possible exciting ideas and explorations.

I remember reading Simone de Beauvoir's ground-breaking book *Second Sex*. She grew up around the time when French women only recently had been allowed to join higher education. This was at the time of Sartre and a lot of other great published philosophers, who incidentally all happened to be male.

Simone de Beauvoir dared to publish her book, perhaps only because it was thought nobody noteworthy would bother reading it. However, Simone wound up changing the minds of men about how women think, and these men wanted more of her writings.

It's said her words also awakened the minds of women. Long-held views around the worth of women were questioned for the first time in history. I read her when I was ten and didn't fully grasp her message, because I had yet to experience the alienations between the sexes.

I read about Eva Peron campaigning for women's rights and Coco Chanel's clothing revolution, as well as others who spoke out for women. I felt a strong connection to the sentiment.

For a long time I wasn't comfortable dressing in a feminine style. I was concerned about being seen in a sexual way, especially because I had large breasts from early on, and this attracted a lot of unwanted attention. At the second high school I went to, they gave us the notion that you had to cover your knees, so you wouldn't draw unwanted attraction.

There was one time I was told by an extended family member that showing my legs was shameful. I really thought about all of this and came to the conclusion that the way I'm physically developed or dressed is not the problem. I told them, "They're legs. They're very handy. It's up to you what you think, but I don't think about them the way you do. I don't need to change who I am." I became even more certain of my self.

My kindness was a perceived as vulnerability to that same extended family member whom I thought I could trust. Had I not been given a voice, I don't think I would have stood up to him that night he strode into my bedroom. I was half naked when he pushed me onto the bed and forced himself on top of me, trying to do things a man should never do to a young girl. I wound up punching him in the face, and he ran from the room. He didn't run because of the force of my punch. He ran because I resisted his aggression. It felt good to stand up for myself. I felt I had delivered an important message: just because he was a grownup, it didn't mean he had rights over a young person.

All of those years they lived next door, he had been grooming me. He found subtle ways to take advantage of me sexually. He creeped all over me with his

CHAPTER 11: Fur Wale

eyes or spied on me in the shower, or bailed me up each time I wandered off alone, or touched me inappropriately. For years he told me, "You will never be as good as my talented and beautiful daughters." He tried convincing me I was unattractive, that I looked like a boy, that I had too many scars, and that no man would want me. His presence was in the daily texture of my life. I was always left not quite certain about what just happened. He would make sure I thought I was wrong in feeling violated. He'd frequently tell my dad that he felt like my father figure and that he would always look after me and protect me, so it kept happening.

At that time we received devastating news that was going to change my family forever. We were told Mum had six months to live, and she might not make it to Christmas. This was too much to take all at once. How could I handle this devastating news, as well as continue to keep the secret about sexual abuse at the hands of the family member?

The brother closest to me in age was my best friend and confidante. I decided to disclose to him what had been happening to me. I craved the idea of my brother rising up against the injustice and wrapping his arms around me protectively. It wasn't easy news to share for many reasons, but especially because this was our time of greatest need, since we were losing the guiding force of our family.

That was brave of you. What was his reaction?

As the last word of the secret escaped my mouth, and I waited for my brother's response, I was surprised by his recoil. I had never seen this look on my brother's face before, yet I knew exactly what it meant. It was too much for him to bear. He regained composure and locked onto my gaze as he said to me "How dare you try to destroy our family!"

A deep, fathomless divide appeared between us. I felt forced to hold it all in. All of a sudden, I was alone in the world. Nothing since then has been able to bring my brother back to me. I learned that being family does not ensure a lifetime bond. One time my dad and a co-worker were talking, and I will never forget dad's words. He said, "If anyone raped my daughter I would take my gun and shoot them, I know I would go to jail, and that's not what my family needs, but I just couldn't let anyone do that to my daughter and get away with it." I wondered why Dad didn't know what was happening to me. Didn't I matter anymore?

What happened with your mum?

The first time we saw mum was after she was in hospital for a period of time. We ran to her, only to stop frightened in our tracks. This wasn't our mother! She sat in a wheelchair, because she'd lost the use of her legs, arms, and hands. She looked fragile. A short, curly brown wig sat on her head. It replaced her straight, long blonde hair. She had no eyebrows and no eyelashes. Her face was pale and puffy, like dough. It wasn't her beautiful face anymore. Intensive chemo had robbed her of her looks.

Whenever dad did night shift, mum would ask me to sleep in bed with her. I always said yes, with only one exception: the night before she died. I didn't know why, but I felt reluctant. She insisted I sit with her and talk a while. Mum said she would miss us. She wanted to know if I would take care of dad and the boys after she left. She spent hours recalling memories and telling me the many things she loved about all of us. She was so brave to talk about dying and leaving us behind. But I always knew Mum had courage.

I remember one night after we discovered someone had slipped hoses through the windows and flooded our house, Mum had grabbed the shotgun from its case and stood on the front porch yelling, "You stay away from my family!" Days before this, a letter threatening payback was placed into our letterbox. The likely suspect at the time was a bloke dad put away in jail who had just been released. I recall observing my mum as I stood to the side of her, out of sight as she'd asked me to. I didn't know how she wasn't scared. In that moment, as my sense of certainty and safety had been taken away by the intrusion, they were returned to me through her courage. I learned how valuable courage is.

The news we were told about Mum was correct. She did not make it to Christmas. She died in her sleep that night at home. Embedded in her brain and wrapped around her thoracic spine were cancerous tumours. That morning, my brother took her a cuppa, and she didn't wake. The ambulance men arrived with a stretcher. Dad took that cue to take his wife's hand to remove her wedding ring and engagement band. As the body bag was laid alongside her, he joined the men in placing her inside. Dad took one last look at the love of his life and kissed her goodbye before he finally pulled up the zipper.

CHAPTER 11: Fur Wale

That must have been hard on you and your family. How did all of you deal with it?

Dad fell apart. He howled like a wild animal. He'd lost his wife and best friend. In his era, men had to soldier on and appear strong. He didn't know how to manage. After we went to bed, he would sit at the breakfast bar, crying into the middle of the night. I would wait a while until I was sure the boys were asleep, and I'd go and sit there with dad. I recognised his appreciation of me through his heaved sigh.

Each night for months he sobbed until collapsing with exhaustion on the bench. He didn't dare to sleep in his bed, where his wife had passed away. I made sure that when Dad woke, his police uniform was ironed, breakfast was made, and he had lunch to take with him, even though I knew he wouldn't eat.

My little brother also took it hard. He had taken mum's dressmaking scissors and shredded all of his clothes. He also smashed everything he owned. He went silent for months. I would snuggle into bed each night with him and read Shakespeare to distract his mind until he fell asleep.

Our other brother moved out to live with his girlfriend in her family home. He went on to create his own family at a distance from us. I needed to talk about Mum's death. I asked, but it seemed everyone wanted to ignore what had just occurred. They were all busying themselves, which I thought was pointless. I wondered how anyone could hold this volume of pain inside without it bursting out, or worse, having it turn on you. In an attempt to make sense of this and to unify our family, especially for my little brother, I took on Mum's role. This was better than feeling complete abandonment, and our family falling apart. This was my life until I went off to Uni.

Weeks later there was a policeman's birthday party that dad felt obliged to go to. He asked me to accompany him. At the party, I was talking to someone and realised dad had left my side. I continued the conversation, thinking he must have gone inside to the bathroom. But when I realised he'd been gone too long, I felt panicked.

I went inside to look for him, opening doors from room to room. I found him in the middle of a room on his knees, with his police handgun shoved into his

Fierce & Fabulous ~ The Feminine Force of Success

mouth directed to blown his brains out. He had a vacant look on his face as if he was done with it and wanted to be gone.

My instant reaction surprised me. I was filled with sharp certainty. Sensing exactly what to say and do, I stood over him and began to negotiate and manage the situation. I insisted he needed to remove the gun *now*. That this was not how it was going to end. Defeated, he slid the pistol out of his mouth but still gripped it tight, and his hand hit the floor. He remained on his knees, until he crumbled into a broken, sobbing lump. I fell to my knees and wrapped my protective arms around him as tears fell out of my eyes. It was in this moment I realised, parents or not, those coping with their own grief may not have anything to offer others in need. Not if they can't take one more drop of pain.

I wondered at the time, *Have I lost everyone?* Through losing my mother, I didn't have anyone to turn to. I didn't know the world anymore, because my life had been shattered. I couldn't trust anything. Even though I understood my family's actions, I was worried that I was no longer important enough for my dad to want to stay alive or for my brother to stay by my side. I was falling into a deep unknown.

You'd been through so much. Did it help when you finally left home?

I moved out of home to go to Uni and study my passions: art, film, and drama. I felt vastly alone at university, even though I was surrounded by people. I remained uncertain of my safety. I felt I'd already made mistakes by letting someone close enough to abuse me, and I had learned that no one could bear hearing about intense pain. I decided to just get on with life and hope that the friends I was making were trustworthy.

There were lots of parties at Uni. Being independent and adventurous meant I was still able to assume a confident manner even when feeling damaged inside. I'd taken to drinking more than I should. One night after a party, I passed out asleep on the floor. I woke, startled to find some stranger with their fingers inside me.

I never slept over at a party again. I instead chose the safety of my bed. But when I was drunk after a get-together, a new male friend asked to sleep over and share my double bed. I thought I would be safe, but I couldn't believe it when I wound up in the same kind of a situation as at that party. Some weeks later, after seeing

CHAPTER 11: Fur Wale

a band with my male best friend, we returned home alone. I was so drunk I ate charcoal out of the fireplace, because I'd heard it soaked up alcohol. I needed to sober up. My head was spinning as I clambered along the hallway, my hands pressed against the wall to find my way. I closed my bedroom door, stripped off my clothes, which was my normal practice, and worked my way under the covers. The next thing I knew a naked body was hovering over the top of me, I desperately wanted to move, but my arms were pinned back forcefully above my head. I tried to remain conscious as I yelled, "No!" It hurt. Tears fell from my eyes as I left my body. I was twenty one. He stole my virginity.

The next party I went to was some years later. I went with a male friend of my younger brother, whose role was to help me feel safe. I loved dancing, so I was on the dance floor when my friend passed a drink to the guys next to me, for them to give it to me. They were teasing me with it, passing it to each other and turning their backs on me. I didn't feel comfortable with their behaviour, so I started to walk off when they said "Hey, take your drink!"

The next thing I knew I was standing alone in the dark street leaning against some car. I panicked. I didn't know how I got there. I wondered why my brain was so messed up. I couldn't control my body. Everything was fluid, whirling. Then, like a hero in a movie, my brother's friend appeared and huddled me to him as he led me back to safety. Back at the party, he sat me down. I thought he'd stay with me, but I must have passed out, and he left.

This next part is the first time I've publicly spoken about this story. It may be hard for you to hear. When I came to, I was in a bathroom bent over the bench, my skirt hitched up. A guy behind me was doing up his pants, and three other guys behind him were doing up their pants and leaving. They were the ones who had no doubt spiked my drink with what I found out later must have been a date rape drug. I got myself outside. Once I found my brother's friend, I gripped his arm and shook violently as I told him to get me out of there.

All of a sudden, a circle formed around us. It was the group of guys again. This time they were laughing and jeering at me, "Look at her. She doesn't even know what a dumb, useless mess she is." As we headed to the car, I recall my protector asking me, "What don't you know?" I turned to tell him but couldn't. When I looked into his eyes, he pulled away from the intense fear he saw there. These last two memories became completely suppressed until some years later.

These experiences would be traumatic for anyone. How did they affect your relationships?

I didn't have luck with boyfriends, either. I looked for love but was incapable of giving it, to the point of demanding they leave in the middle of the night. My relationships weren't short, they were drawn out. Years would pass, and the guy wouldn't leave me. Many of them were good guys, but I wore them down. They would become possessive and angry at me for the crumbs of love they felt forced to live off. I just couldn't bring myself to open up. Two of the relationships turned violent, manipulative. I was even date raped by one. I chose to stay single for a long time after that.

There was a time when you wanted to save everyone, but they didn't want help. Did it ever come to a head? Did you wind up seeking help for the trauma you experienced?

Eventually, dad was successful in taking his life. You should have seen his funeral. I arrived late, because of my youngest brother delaying us. When we got out of the car, we couldn't believe it. The front lawn was full of people. We assumed they were waiting to go in, but they were unable to fit in.

Dad was my hero, but I hadn't realised he was a hero to hundreds of people. Maybe I shouldn't have been surprised. He was an extraordinary man, and I don't think he realised. He made an impression upon those he met, even casually. Dad was that rare policeman who talked to the heart of the person first. He was one of the undercover detectives investigating the shady characters represented in the television series *Underbelly*.

The funeral parlour had opened the adjoining room to accommodate the people that were pouring in. No chair was empty. It was standing-room only, plus the crowd of people on the lawn. All to bid respect to Senior Sergeant Detective David Cameron Wale. I had wondered if they knew he'd hung himself from the tree in the front of his property.

My little brother's coping mechanism for years was alcohol. From Friday after work until bed early hours Monday, he was a full-time alcoholic as an outlet for grief, and he could easily turn violent defending his self-worth. The only person he had left was me, and I had promised him I would never abandon him, even after he'd turned on me.

CHAPTER 11: Fur Wale

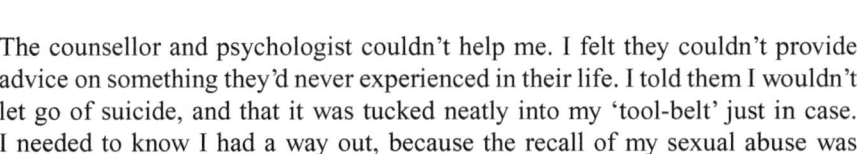

The counsellor and psychologist couldn't help me. I felt they couldn't provide advice on something they'd never experienced in their life. I told them I wouldn't let go of suicide, and that it was tucked neatly into my 'tool-belt' just in case. I needed to know I had a way out, because the recall of my sexual abuse was almost unbearable. Knowing I had suicide as my aid offered a modicum of support. It was my last bastion of self control.

Secrets poison you, and post-traumatic stress became my personal living hell. One evening, I decided that was it. I wanted out. I was going take my life. There was no more hope left for me. I was all alone in the world and nothing was changing. I felt tortured by my past and pretending to be happy was no life worth living. On my walk home, I unshackled my possessions and gave them to the homeless people on the street. My jewellery, my money, the contents of my bag, my coat, my shoes, and finally the bag. Behind a closed door in my bedroom, I put on music and tidied my room. On my desk I set out the lethal dose of drugs I had purchased, which was easy to do on the back streets of St Kilda, and wrote a note. I knew I was ready, because I didn't cry. I sat for a moment in meditation. A slither of ease entered as I heard the words in my head, *Time to go home.* I didn't know at the time what that meant, other than it had become a constant companion of mine.

At that moment something landed against my door. I jumped up. There was sobbing. I stood silent. It was my brother, and I didn't want him to know I was here. The pause was intensely long. Then he let out a cry for help. "Sissy...I need you!" That broke me. My brother...my promise I had made years earlier. It was an incredible turning point. I thought, *Why haven't I made that promise to myself? I also deserve not be abandoned, don't I?*

I was exhausted, I didn't want to be hard, closed off, and empty anymore. I wanted to know what I thought, to feel feelings. I needed to know my place in the world. I wanted to genuinely connect with what I was doing instead of going through the motions, numb.

Once I realised I was gripped by the intensity of feeling like a victim, I decided I would make it okay that I wasn't okay, and that became my start to not being a victim anymore.

It was better than feeling completely powerless. I had been focussed on what I didn't want and who I wasn't. I filled my mind with 'I wants' that I was convinced I didn't deserve and therefore would never be mine. No wonder I felt stuck and devastated, seeing life as less than. I was a slave to my thinking. My beliefs made it so. I had been bouncing between feeling triggered by memories and limited by my rigidly held beliefs of being worthless. I longed for peace to comfort me.

For no immediately apparent reason, I thought, *How did I learn to swim?* As I let the words of my memory transcribe through the pen to my journal, they formed feelings of trust. A sense of ease that I had forgotten flooded me. When I was two years of age, I lay cradled in my dad's big, gentle hands, resting against his chest. He was waist deep in the pool and slowly lowered me to the surface of the water, his eyes never leaving mine. A warm, pleasant feeling lapped around me as his hands slowly left my side. I was held buoyant by the water and the air in my lungs. In this silence, I felt free. I thought I had lost myself in the shattered pieces of my life, but recalling this memory brought me back to a time when I knew exactly who I was. When I felt safe in the world. Recalling the moment let me know I could feel this again…I could be this.

Having made my promise not to abandon myself, I decided I would give myself three months to do something different and make life work for me. And if those three months worked, I would give myself another three doing what it takes, and another three. I had to purposefully transform my outlook, because the way I'd been looking at my life was destroying me. I needed new ways of seeing the world.

First, I decided I was going to feel happy by seeing life as more than rather than *less than*. I had been looking at life as being a kind of hell. What if this was as good as it gets? Couldn't I then find goodness in it? I became responsible for my own happiness and my own wellbeing and stopped expecting it was owed to me. I understood the choices and decisions I made moment to moment directly impacted the quality of my day. What I gave power to had power over me. I learned that we attract our dominant thoughts, feelings, and observations, and what we practice becomes our outcome.

So, instead of digging around in The Story of my life, I decided to accept that the 'horror story' was a part of me, at least for the time being. I allowed myself to see that 'what had been done to me' did not make me unloved, unwanted, less-

CHAPTER 11: Fur Wale

than, damaged, shameful, or wrong. I realised that vulnerability and anxiety, to a degree, were a part of life. I assessed the percentage of it I was willing to live with and chose to look forward to dissolving the rest. I gave my home a complete makeover by throwing out all of the reminders of my past. I redecorated. Everything in my home needed to inspire me.

These decisions released a great deal of resistance in my mind and body. I was letting go of The Story tearing me down and chose instead to let it grow me up and inspire me daily. This gave me some peace and clarity in place of trying to barricade myself from being hurt. From this place of allowing, I was able to pick up my shattered beliefs and ask, "Do I need this?"

It was just like trying on a new outfit to see if it still fit and discarding any that didn't. While trying them out in the world, I kept only beliefs that served me well. I longed for the kindness I once shared that opened me up to the world of others. That was *me*, and I wanted me back, even though I was scared, because kindness is an exchange that invites unpredictable responses.

To feel safe and survive this, I needed a plan to deal with the risks. I had to gain control and feel certainty. From here on I would choose carefully what I would experience. I stepped out into the world when I felt confident. I would leave before discomfort set in. I prepared comments I would say during conversations and for escaping the situation. In place of being focussed on the anxiety, I practiced expecting the best out of each occurrence.

To be able to make each moment better, I would list in my mind all of the things I appreciated. My day would start with me writing in my journal, and I would also put my day to rest by writing the actions I discovered had worked, because I was building my life skills tool belt. I deliberately constructed each day like that. Sometimes it was a challenge to see the good, but I never silently suffered my way through anything again.

I was releasing the pain without having to delve into it, without unnecessarily re-triggering myself. There was a new me emerging and evolving from a new way of thinking. I was learning to set boundaries and speak up for myself again, even if it might offend someone. I was recreating myself into the person I wanted to be, so I changed my name from Jennifer to my nickname. From that point on, I have been known as Fur.

We all share a sense that we are living lives restricted by the belief that the life we really want escapes us. Such thinking in itself limits us. There are straightforward life tools that when practiced, enable us to overcome this feeling of being stuck and open the doors to our success. No matter what you have experienced, or what you have not yet experienced, there is always a way to achieve your vision.

What would be your message to others who've had traumatic experiences in their own lives?

Knowing now what I didn't know then, I'm here to let you know, without a doubt, it is possible to claim your life back from wherever you are! Even when you feel you've been thrown off your path, *you are still on it.* It's the contrasting experiences, along with the acceptance of them, that creates depth and insight. It will inspire and empower you.

All things are possible when we continue to practice clarity of focus and assess our beliefs and resourcefulness. Your most valuable resources are having *hope*, a *vision*, and *inspired action*.

My experiences have become profoundly pivotal to the direction my life has taken. I have a burning drive within me to connect with others in order to witness their inherent worth. My desire as a public figure is to offer everything I'm equipped with to inspire and empower, and this extends to all communities, especially to all women.

We are lucky to be living in this day and age, but there's still an inherent issue surrounding women feeling *less than* and unequal to males. For example, rape is still a weapon.

Maya Angelo wrote a book in 1969 called *I know Why the Caged Bird Sings*. The core message is about the agony of not sharing your story. It's true that talking is transformative. I think that's particularly potent for *all women*. I want you to step up and claim your history. You stand here today as you are because of your life stories. When you own your story, you open yourself to the pearls of wisdom held inside the struggle. This is how you know your authentic self. The clarity, wisdom, self-knowledge, and determination gained out of it, is true success. There is an empowering shift in our emotional, mental, and physical states when we own our life stories. And there is always someone who will benefit and come away inspired and empowered.

CHAPTER 11: Fur Wale

Women have all of the makings of great speakers, because they're the most influential role models we have. Women are naturally great storytellers. We have unbridled dreams and passion to share. Most of all, we deliver our messages as a gift. It's just that we tend to step back and often attribute success to a combination of factors, unlike men who will often body step into the limelight. This is why women benefit from regular participation in activities that open them up to performing authentically and surrounding themselves with role models.

As a result, I highly recommend joining a community theatre group and participating in movement classes such as dance, yoga, and *Feldenkrais*. We are better people when exposed to concepts that expand our mind and encompass others' perspectives. Become fuelled by daily inspiration, and consistently seek like-minded connections. Regularly participate in activities that surround you with excellent role models. Attend as many workshops as you can that will broaden you. In Melbourne there's always some great free workshop going on. Just go and network and practice speaking to people. Take speaker training to learn and hone skills or participate in any other activity that inspires you to be fully yourself and enables you to communicate authentically. It's important for us to learn to use our voice to deliver our messages the way we intend them to be received.

It takes effort to live an exceptional life. Don't be lazy, and do something every day that speaks to your authenticity and your dream. It will be worth it!

How important do you feel mentors are?

I believe everyone needs a mentor. In fact, they need more than one. Mentors can be people who are already getting the results you want. We need them to feel inspired, to gain insight, keep focussed, and maintain momentum. Successful people can provide this. The ones to focus on are those who live in their authentic presence and keep evolving. Take Oprah Winfrey. She lives to inspire others through living an inspired life. Oprah's story is relatable. She had to step out on her own and have her voice heard. As I was watching her show one day, Oprah said to a young woman who'd been raped, "It's not your fault. You didn't do anything wrong." It was like a battering ram had crashed through the walls of my numbness, and there was an outburst of feelings. I finally received the words I needed to hear, so I could move on. Sometimes there are specific words relating to our situation we need to hear. This is why it's beneficial to keep tapped into any information that can broaden us. I find mentors through books, workshops, by following successful people's stories, and spending time with successful people. I have experienced mentors for each aspect of my business.

Tell me about SHE Talks®.

The customised speaker training and development platform for women I have developed is called SHE Talks®. SHE stands for *Speak. Hear. Empower.* It's all about women deciding in what capacity they need and want to share their voice. A complete range of information is available that's suitable for all women and all situations. SHE Talks® is especially valuable to the leaders of small enterprises. The role of these entrepreneurs is to deliver their message as the expert, with complete authenticity and impact, to as broad a market as possible.

It's also especially important for Gen Y. They're savvy and very switched on. They know so much more, because they have access to vast information and technology. To the Gen Y readers of the book I say, "You are our global citizens out there inspiring the world." There are young women who want to own their own success and walk this earth in a way that shows they know they rightfully belong here. In fact, more women need to feel that. And there's the stay-at-home mums wanting the opportunity to get out into their neighbourhood and speak about matters that concern them, their families, and their community. They want not only to be a great role model as a mum, they want their community to thrive. These women are the leaders of conversations at schools, at Rotary, at family events, and as inspirational mentors for their own children, as well as others.

I provide the A-Z of speaking publicly. I also provide information for running projects that enable women and young girls to set up projects themselves. This module creates a good base for those seeking to have the knowledge or confidence. Can you imagine mums starting a project with their children as an activity for the day?

There's an even bigger call for women speakers at small and large events, now more than ever before in history! Right now we need the depth and wisdom women have to offer. This is why the SHE Talks® Network of Inspired Women is so important. I invite you to come participate in workshops and hear me speak. Please come share your stories as a way of allowing SHE Talks® to move in the direction it's most needed. Align with the authentic conversations being held,

CHAPTER 11: Fur Wale

and share with your network your wisdom and inspired action. Inspire fellow women. The more women come together, the more we can support each other in what we're doing to create shifts in the world. I started out certain of my place in the world. Then life happened, and I became afraid to be myself. I chose to risk being me even when people said, "who does she think she is?", because being authentically *you* is the most important thing in the world.

Here's to creating our life, defining moments, beautiful epiphanies, and incredible connections. I look forward to meeting you!

About SHE Talks® by Fur Wale

#NetworkOfInspiredWomen

SHETalks@outlook.com

Launched in 2015, SHE Talks® is a business that creates new benchmarks and offers speaker training created and delivered by a woman. Fur Wale has expertly customised a platform for women seeking to deliver talks with confidence and impact. The focus is on inspiring and empowering women to utilise their authentic presence and share their unique messages with others, whether it's within their businesses, community, or family events. SHE Talks® aims to understand and advance women as individuals by embracing their diverse ways of being and performing. Authentic presence emerges as one of the dominant factors influencing a woman's success.

CHAPTER 11: Fur Wale

The training is reasonably priced and delivers a fast, yet thorough, experience for learning public speaking in all capacities. A balance of theoretical and practical applications provides a most immersive and transformative learning environment. Interactive E-learning, with clear step-by-step tutorials, engages multi-sensory learning content. Personality profiling, quizzes, feedback, checklists, mentor assessments, print outs, and support are all part of the package.

Experience is fast tracked using prompts, activities, and challenges combined with abundant speaking opportunities. Professional, state-of-the art rehearsal spaces are provided where it's possible to be reviewed by your peers and obtain the footage. As a member of the speaker's hub, you will have ample access to networking events and job opportunities. Join the online chat in the forum and connect with others with similar aspirations. Invaluable resources can be sourced in the vault and only accessed by members. Ongoing support is provided after the training.

Each participant creates their own course outcome by choosing which modules fit their needs and wants. Flexibility is key. Duration depends upon how many modules the participant chooses to complete. Small businesses and entrepreneurs can benefit by maximising their time with achievable daily components that fast track learning and experience.

SHE Talks® training understands that women inherently seek to be authentic. Training for public speaking often is delivered by men, corporate in style, and based on pre-determined gestures and tonality. As women, we deliver our messages as a gift, and to do this we need to be unashamedly ourselves. We are great storytellers. Mothers, sisters, aunties, and grandmothers all have something unique and powerful to contribute.

SHE Talks® was inspired by the desire to have a platform from which to share stories and effect change. Fur Wale brings her network and all of her professional and life experiences to the training. Her vision is to enable women to change the conversations of our culture, because what we say or do not say will affect generations to come. She is committed to inspiring and empowering women, and as a consequence, their community, partner, and children.

SHE Talks® is essentially a Network of Inspired Women who Speak, Hear, Empower.

Fur Wale has been invited to speak at many events with over a hundred people, including local government, the mayor, and council. She delivers creative projects, all with one key purpose – to define what living on your own terms really looks like. While the topics she is requested to deliver may vary, what the audience is always seeking remains the same – to 'GET IT'. Fur Wale always gifts her audience with the big Aha.

~ Sandy Joffe, CEO, PPCG

CHAPTER 12

Kelly Fletcher

"Your greatest adversary is also your greatest teacher."

Iyanla Vanzant

CHAPTER 12: Kelly Fletcher

CHAPTER TWELVE
Kelly Fletcher

Kelly is a Holistic Healer, Transformational Coach, and Workshop Leader specialising in Forensic Healing, NLP, Time Line Therapy, and Hypnotherapy

I Met Kelly at a women's forum organised by Di Bell in Horsham, where we both spoke. I was so impressed with her presentation that I wanted to know her story. When we got together, we spoke about life, love, children, social change, the issues young people are facing in our community, and what we could do to help them.

WARNING: Sensitive topics regarding sexual abuse and suicide.

Tell me about your early life.

My story begins on the 5th September, 1970, when I was born in the small country town of Dimboola. I had two siblings, Geoff who was a year and a half older, and Mark who was nine years younger. I grew up in a working-class family. My dad worked most of his life on the railways, and my mum for the most part was a cleaner. Money was reasonably tight, and we often lived from pay to pay. My first home was an old weatherboard that needed a lot of work. We were fortunate that when I was about nine we moved into a newly established housing commission home.

Growing up in a small community had its benefits. I was lucky to be involved in many local sports, such as basketball, tennis, netball, and swimming. I felt safe and often spent time at the local common building cubby houses.

I had a close connection with my paternal grandma, and I spent many Sunday nights with extended family playing cards. My grandma was a strong woman who as a single parent raised nine children. She also lost a set of twins. My Grandma taught me the power of independence and strength as a woman.

When I was around ten, I had my first job delivering the local paper. I remember those icy cold mornings well. At thirteen I obtained a part-time job at the neighbourhood supermarket and waitressed at the local hotel. One thing my parents taught me well was a good work ethic.

Alcohol was certainly an accepted culture in our family and community. Weekend sessions were a regular occurrence. My dad's view on life was, "If you're going to do anything, I'd rather you did it under my roof." I liked this philosophy at the time, and I'm sure it enabled me to make positive decisions for myself, but at the age of thirteen I was able to drink alcohol and smoke cigarettes at home. The acceptance of this as normal behaviour certainly had an impact on my upbringing, but it's led me to make different decisions for my own family.

What would you say are your defining moments, and what did they lead you to do?

There are a number of defining moments in my life that I believe have shaped the person I am today. The first was the death of my close friend, Chris, who sadly ended his life on the 3rd November 1985. Chris was twenty at the time and had experienced a difficult upbringing. At a young age he'd lost his own father to what everyone believed was a suicidal drowning.

I remember the moment I found out like it was only yesterday. I was home alone, and Chris rang me to say how much he loved me and to say his goodbyes. We talked for what seemed like hours, but nothing I could say would make him change his mind. He had a plan to end his life. He had a gun at his side with every intention to use it.

I felt complete powerlessness knowing this would be the last conversation I would ever have with Chris. I knew this in my heart, because I had been with him a few months before when he'd attempted suicide. On this occasion I had walked the streets of Dimboola with him whilst he repeatedly made cuts to his wrists with jagged pieces of tin. On that day I was able to get him to the hospital, but on the night of his death, I was too far away. He was in Melbourne alone, with no one I could ring to get help for him. I didn't even have his address to send the police to and didn't think of this at the time. I just had the knowledge that nothing I did or said would change his mind. He truly wanted to end his sadness and his life.

CHAPTER 12: Kelly Fletcher

After I hung up the phone, I curled up in the foetal position and sobbed hysterically. My parents arrived home to find me still in this position. I could hardly speak. When I was finally able to tell them, my dad got angry Chris had upset me so much. I didn't sleep a lot that night, and the next morning I awoke to the news that he was dead. The days that followed were a fog, and the funeral was heart wrenching. Chris's death rocked the community and particularly my peer group. I remember often visiting the gravesite and talking to him in an effort to search for answers to life.

In the last letter I received from Chris before his suicide, he expressed his fears of returning to juvenile detention and said there was no way he was going to let that happen. He explained how he'd been drunk and abusive towards the police, and they in turn assaulted him.

What I remember most about Chris is his compassion, his zest for life, and his big smile. He would always sign off his letters with *Keep Smilin'*. Chris taught me about the power of creating and choosing endless opportunities.

There were a lot of people in my life who attempted or committed suicide. Prior to Chris, my brother Geoff cut his wrists with a broken bottle after breaking up with his girlfriend. I'm not sure whether his intention was to end the pain or end his life. Geoff had moved out of home at age sixteen to work on a property in a small farming community nearby. Being the eldest child, he had a lot of pressure on him, and his relationship with dad was always strained. We were close growing up, as we shared many of the same friends and would spend a lot of time hanging out together. Geoff taught me the power of letting go of old hurts.

My best friend, Jodie, had also cut her wrists, but I believe this was more an attempt to rid herself of the emotional pain she was feeling inside than an attempt on her life. She had experienced so much hurt and pain in her young life. Jodie taught me the power of gratitude.

My boyfriend, Dale, made his first attempt at suicide by taking an overdose of pills. I was hurt and saddened. He struggled for many years with schizophrenia and later ended his life by hanging in October of 2005, when he lost his struggle. Dale's death rocked those who knew him well. It showed that at any age, life can become too hard if you don't know how to access the right support.

What I remember the most about Dale is his beautiful smile, his love for the ocean and fishing, and some of the crazy, funny things he used to do that would always put a smile on my face. Dale was my first true love, and I will always have a connection to him. I'm sure he and Chris have met somewhere in another life to talk about old times.

Every time I hear Cold Chisel's "Flame Trees" it reminds me of Dale and takes me back to a time when he first moved to Melbourne to work. Every time he'd leave again, I would play "Flame Trees" to feel closer to him. Dale taught me the power of connection.

During my adolescence, many friends attempted suicide. It was almost as though it had become acceptable to give up hope. Many of the boys lived dangerously and would risk their lives driving fast and crazy in their cars. I'm sure they did believe they were infallible and had no fear of death.

The next defining moment in my life also happened just before my fifteenth birthday. I've thought long and hard about whether or not to talk about this, because it's private and hard to put into words. But to be true to myself and my journey, I feel it's right to include it.

I was sexually assaulted by a stranger. I was a virgin at the time, and this event took away my innocence and choices. It left me feeling completely powerless and impacted my self-esteem and self-worth for many years to come. I never told anyone at the time and have buried it ever since. It was only in the past couple of years that I've truly started to deal with its impact on my life. I achieved this through doing self-development courses such as the You can Heal Your Life workshop by Louise Hay and natural therapies such as NLP, Time Line Therapy, and hypnosis.

My survival tool was my ability to journal how I was feeling, as well as to create poems to express these feelings. My journaling allowed me to release my emotions as they arose and to feel like I was talking to someone. I find it so much easier, even today, to write how I truly feel rather than to say it out loud.

My peer group was also vital to my survival, especially my best friend Jodie. Even if we're far apart, no matter what's going on in our lives, we know we're only a phone call away from each other.

CHAPTER 12: Kelly Fletcher

These people have led me to make many big decisions about my life. I knew from a young age I was destined to work in a field where I could help people. At school I wanted to either be a teacher, social worker, or police officer. My careers teacher smartly advised me to go to university to open up my options, even though by Year 10 I knew the police force was the choice I was going to make. I completed my Bachelor of Arts through Deakin University, two years off campus and one year on, due to financing my own way through. The year I spent in Geelong, I travelled back to Dimboola every week to work my two jobs.

Living in Geelong was interesting and challenging. I lived with my aunty and uncle, who I have immense gratitude for. But this was a trying time for them, as my cousin Glenda, who was almost like a sister to me, became involved with the wrong group of people through her boyfriend and developed a significant drug addiction. It was difficult seeing the pain my aunty and uncle experienced, but I felt that in some way my presence helped them deal with this situation.

As soon as I completed my degree I was ready to join the police force. I trained hard. I ran every day and stuck to a strict regimen of weight training, swimming, and bike riding. Being a solid girl, I had to work hard to maintain my weight under the height/weight ratio. It was a constant battle. I often lived for periods of time on steamed veggies and fruit. My friends, Allan and Jane, were both instrumental in helping me train and keep on track, and for that I thank them very much.

My dad was a huge support during this time. He built an obstacle course in our back paddock that was a simulation of the course I had to get through to pass the physical test. I would practise daily getting over the wall and hurdle. This was a challenge for me, being of short stature, but I was determined and persistent not to let any obstacle stand in the way of my dream to become a police officer.

I applied to both South Australia and Victoria and was given offers to both within weeks of each other. I chose South Australia, because the process and people seemed friendlier. I had never been keen to live in Melbourne, as it always seemed like a big, scary city after growing up in a small country town. My boyfriend at the time was also thinking of moving to Adelaide for football, so it all seemed like the right choice. My dad taught me the power of following your dreams.

I was a police officer in South Australia for almost fifteen years. I began my career at Glenelg, where I worked for two years before I went to work in the city of Adelaide on patrols. I worked there for about three years.

One of the early jobs as a patrol officer in Adelaide was a tasking to a middle-aged male at the Rotunda who had a knife to his juggler and was threatening to kill himself. I acted on intuition and took the lead role of talking to him for about two hours. My partner then successfully capsicum sprayed him to obtain the knife and safely got him to the hospital where he was cared for.

This incident brought back a lot of my emotions about Chris's death. I rang Jodie when I got home from my shift and spent hours talking to her before going to sleep. I voiced my immense frustration at my colleagues who had no empathy or understanding and jokingly stated, "If he came at me with the knife I would have shot him," knowing full well the man had no intention of harming anyone but himself.

A few months later my sergeant called me into the office and gave me a copy of a letter. It was to the commissioner of police from that man. It went something like this:

I didn't care much about my life that night, but thank God the female police officer did, and I really want to thank her and the male officer for caring enough about me to save my life.

Somehow, this letter made everything okay.

During my time in Adelaide I completed my Associate Diploma in Justice Administration to qualify to the rank of Senior Sergeant. But I knew that I didn't want to be a patrol officer forever, so I went back to Uni to complete further study in psychology. I thought I would take the path of becoming a police psychologist. Human behaviour was always my fascination. But I soon discovered it was going to take me another six years of part-time study whilst working full-time to complete my honours and master's. And after all of that I would start on a pay a lot lower than I earned on the police force, so I decided not to take this path.

The next defining moment came when I made a rapid decision to move to the country. I had been moving from rental house to rental house, and I was sick

CHAPTER 12: Kelly Fletcher

of it. Then I was told the house I'd just moved into was going to be sold, and I would have to move again. I rang up country transfers to see what my options were. I didn't know much about country South Australia, as Adelaide had been the only place I'd been, apart from the highway between Adelaide and Dimboola. They told me I could move to Whyalla in three weeks if I liked. I said to give me six. I'd never been to Whyalla and had no idea what to expect. The benefit of working in the country as a police officer at that time was that the rent was so cheap, about twenty-seven dollars a week, and the police force bore the cost of moving you. It all seemed like a great option for me.

So on 5/11/1997, I moved to Whyalla. I recall this date distinctly, because it was Jodie's birthday. I'm not sure if she's forgiven me yet for moving that day, as she was living in Adelaide at the time, and we spent a lot of time together.

I loved the Whyalla community and felt welcomed from the moment I arrived. I quickly immersed myself in local sports and social events with other police officers. It was a fantastic lifestyle for a young, single woman, and I had many fun nights at the local hotel.

It's ironic that the first death message I ever delivered as a young Constable was to a father whose son had committed suicide. He fainted in shock and fell backwards. It was fortunate it was onto a couch and not through the window behind. Death messages, along with dealing with dead bodies, were horrible parts of the job no police officer enjoys.

I had a passion for working with victims and was sure my next career move was going to be to the Sexual Assault Unit back in Adelaide. I completed all of the courses needed, but I think fate took its course again. If you were a female officer in the country, it was a regular occurrence to be called out to deal with rapes and child sexual abuse. I quickly learnt this work touched buttons in me I didn't want touched, and hearing these sad stories all of the time would play on my mind. This caused me to change direction once again.

I was looking for a field that offered day shift, because I struggled for many years with insomnia and constant sickness due to the constant stress of shift work. I decided to become a police prosecutor. I did complete the prosecutor's course, which I must say was pretty gruelling but enjoyable and challenging at the same time. I worked in this field for two years, but I had a personality clash with the sergeant in charge of the unit and found it difficult to work with him.

During this time, I met the love of my life and true soul mate, Fletch, whom I married on 27/10/2001 at the foreshore of Whyalla. At a Police 70's night, I was trying to set him up with my good friend. It seems his mates, most of whom were my work colleagues, had a similar idea, only they were trying to set him up with me. Well, I guess I was the lucky one that night, because I knew from that moment on we were going to be together for many years to come. I felt that instant connection you only hear about in romantic movies.

The next moment that defined and changed our lives forever came along soon after, with the birth of our first and only child, Dylan. He was born on 22/12/2002. It would take a whole book to talk about the lessons Dylan has brought into our lives.

When he was about five and a half months old, I returned to work full time as the Youth and Community Officer for Mid-West Local Service Area. Whilst on maternity leave I was successful in obtaining the position. A wise friend pointed out that with a young child, I shouldn't return to the stress I'd been experiencing in my role as prosecutor. I had tried to resolve the differences between me and my sergeant, to no avail.

I grew to love this job with great passion. I got to work with the young and old in a caring and compassionate way, whilst utilising my organisational skills to implement a range of amazing programs for the community. I loved the strong connections to a wide range of community groups and organisations and found my passion for working with young people.

In May, 2005 I was awarded the South Australian Police Officer of the Year award, something I didn't expect but was humbled to receive. It made all of the long hours seem worthwhile, and it was amazing to get recognition and support from the wider community. The town even held a mayoral reception in my honour for the work I'd done in collaboration with many organisations in the town. I loved instigating, developing, and coordinating a range of youth programs in the region, including the Whyalla Basketball Program that was successful in winning a National Crime Prevention award.

The next defining moment in my life was when my mum became ill. The doctors had discovered two aneurisms in her brain when she was hospitalised for a kidney infection. She was to undergo major brain surgery to have the aneurisms clamped and drained. Dylan was young at the time, work was hectic,

CHAPTER 12: Kelly Fletcher

and I wasn't able to get the time off to travel to Victoria to be with her for her operation. There was that feeling of powerlessness again, when I thought I was going to lose her. It was difficult obtaining information from a distance, and she took a long time to come out of the operation. My mum taught me the power of building resilience.

It was due to this event I started to think about moving home. I knew I needed to be closer to my family, and it was important for Dylan to get to know his grandparents before it was too late. I thought about this for some time before telling my husband. There was even more pressure when I was given a job offer the same day I sent my résumé. My husband had been born and bred in Whyalla, and I was asking him to give up a lot. He couldn't quite grasp my sudden need to move states, and there was a time when I didn't know if our marriage was going to get through it. I just knew it was something I had to do no matter what.

So in June, 2006 we moved to Horsham, and it's turned out to be one of the best decisions we've ever made. Don't get me wrong. There have been challenges, especially in the beginning, but the path upon which it has taken our family has proven to be truly amazing.

I initially worked at Grampians Community Health Centre as a drug and alcohol counsellor, but something didn't feel right about this role for me. I needed structure and organisation after the police force, so I applied and won the position as Youth Justice Advanced Case Worker at the Department of Human Services in October, 2006. This position utilised all of the skills I had developed in my time as a police officer. It was working with young people who were experiencing challenges in their lives. Many of them came from troubled backgrounds and had experienced a great deal of trauma, grief, and loss that sounded a lot like Chris's story.

I spent five and a half years in this role. I was passionate about it, and I loved the challenges it brought. But as I developed my personal life and took the path of a natural approach towards health and wellness, my values and beliefs started to diverge from the department I was working for. I felt an internal conflict whenever a young person came in experiencing mental health issues. I had a whole wealth of information that would help them, but the system I was bound to would not accept holistic healing if it wasn't part of a medical model. They advocated psychiatry and medication.

Around December of 2012 I had four clients who were experiencing significant suicidal thoughts. One ended up hospitalised as a result of an attempted overdose. I had a five- week holiday shortly after this incident, and it allowed me time to reassess my life. I decided it was time to move on. It's amazing how much clearer my thinking had become whilst I was away from work. I applied for the position as Wellbeing Officer at Horsham College, and was blessed to be offered this role. I feel I'm utilising all I've learnt to help young people through challenging times.

In February, 2012, whilst at a convention in Adelaide called Endless Opportunities, fate again took its course. I was sitting alone in a café waiting for my lunch, when Jim Patterson, the lead singer of The Borders, walked in. I had met Jim a few times before and loved his music. We talked, and he told me of the loss of his son to suicide. Because of this short conversation, I finally came to my purpose for being on this earth.

When I went back to my room, I started writing and couldn't stop. I knew I had to build awareness in the wider community about suicide, mental health, grief and loss, and substance abuse. I also had to make people aware there are many other ways of dealing with these issues that didn't involve taking prescribed psychotropic drugs.

How did you go about that?

My personal journey to better health and wellness begins in May, 2008, after attending a Hidden Dangers seminar on ADHD by Parenting Strategist Lillian Reekie. As a family we embarked on a new lifestyle initially to help Dylan, only to discover it transformed my life, as well as my husband's.

There were four key areas the Hidden Dangers seminar taught me that impacted on my health and wellbeing: diet, chemical toxicity, nutrition, and self-esteem. I initially implemented the Prince Alfred Hospital Elimination Diet for all of my family. This proved to make a major difference in my life. I discovered I had food intolerances that were impacting significantly on my health. I transformed my household from a toxic chemical waste ground to one of chemically safe products.

I then added in good quality nutritionals from a reputable company. I gradually built up this nutritional base as I saw more and more benefits from taking

CHAPTER 12: Kelly Fletcher

supplements. I was initially reluctant to spend money on them, until I saw the amazing difference it was making to my health, in particular the nutritional support I was using to balance my hormones. It enabled me to cope so much better with life.

I later learnt the importance of completing a heavy metal detox, which combined with bicom treatment, gave me more amazing benefits for my health. It also reduced my food intolerances.

In terms of self-esteem, I started with the Hidden Dangers subliminal CDs but advanced to a wide range of personal development books and CDs. I've found that the more I learn the more I want to know. I'm a particular fan of Louise Hay's *You can Heal your Life* and describe her workshops as better than fifty therapy sessions. I love her work so much. After the transformations it made for me, I went on to become a Louise Hay Workshop Leader and Life Coach. Shortly after this I also competed my training in forensic healing, and it, too, was life changing and transformational. In 2014 I completed my master practitioner training in NLP, coaching, hypnosis, and Time Line Therapy.

How important do you feel mentors are?

Lillian taught me the power of having an amazing mentor. My family is so grateful for Lillian's mentoring for the past seven years. It has truly changed our lives. I choose to mentor three young girls, and I love it. They have taught me the power of being a mentor for someone else. Thank you, Emily, Erin, and Jenelle.

You've shared many defining moments, but you've had one that happened more recently. Tell me about it.

The next defining moment in my life came in 2014 when I experienced significant conflict at work with my line manager. I obviously hadn't learned my lesson when I was on the police force, so I needed to repeat the pattern. The stress of this conflict had become so severe it made me physically and emotionally unwell. As a result I chose to take extended leave. This would allow me to pursue my studies and start my own business. Little did I know how much this training would transform my life.

I took a practitioner course. What happens when you do personal development is that it brings your issues or problems to the surface, so you're forced to deal with them one way or another. Boy, was this true for me. After completing practitioner, I became aware that my marriage was no longer healthy, and I needed to do something about it. I had probably pushed down my needs in this relationship for some time, as you do when you have a young child with challenges who takes up a lot of your energy. My husband had always been like my best friend, but there were things missing in our relationship that didn't seem repairable. Our ideas around parenting had always caused conflict, and Dylan was good at activating these buttons to create conflict in our relationship. What child doesn't like the attention of both parents, after all?

So upon returning from my training, I instigated a marriage separation. To others this seemed sudden, but the marriage hadn't been right for some time. Fletch taught me the power of forgiveness of myself and others.

This took me on a whole new journey. I was faced with significant financial stress as I returned to a part-time single wage. This was made even more difficult, because I'd made commitments pre-separation I was unable to change. It also meant I had to return to my job to ensure I had a secure income. It's unfortunate that the situation had not been resolved with my line manager, so what resulted next changed my perspective on life.

During this time I also met a lot of amazing people who inspired me, but one in particular who stands out is Adam. He's a successful businessman, despite his own personal journey of pain. He taught me the power of inspiring others and building a successful team, as well as being humble in your wealth and giving back to the community. Adam continues to inspire people every day to be the best that they can be, and I hope I will be able to do the same.

I returned to work in July, 2014, but the night before I had anxiety like I'd never experienced before, because I had not resolved the situation with my line manager. For the next month I struggled to go to work on very little sleep. I had extreme anxiety, complete loss of belief in myself, financial stress, and grief over the loss of my relationship. I was also dealing with Dylan, who was struggling with the separation and experiencing such high anxiety, he refused to go to school. My world came tumbling down in a big crash during the time I'd been on such a journey of personal transformation. What I believe happened for

CHAPTER 12: Kelly Fletcher

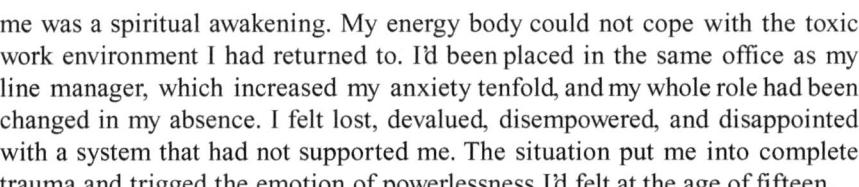

me was a spiritual awakening. My energy body could not cope with the toxic work environment I had returned to. I'd been placed in the same office as my line manager, which increased my anxiety tenfold, and my whole role had been changed in my absence. I felt lost, devalued, disempowered, and disappointed with a system that had not supported me. The situation put me into complete trauma and trigged the emotion of powerlessness I'd felt at the age of fifteen.

I soon crashed completely and reached the point of fight or flight. I froze. My cognitive brain would not function. I felt there was no hope for living, and that my life as I knew it was over. I was never going to be able to work again and believed I had nothing to offer the world or any skills to talk of. I became housebound, as I would experience severe panic attacks whenever I left the house and had an intense fear of becoming homeless.

At points I wanted to give up on life and didn't know how I was going to continue to live with the anxiety and pain I was going through. Interestingly enough, I found true friendships and the value of family during this time. My biggest support came from my brothers, my parents, a few close friends, Fletch, and especially Dylan. He's given me so many lessons, but the most valuable has been the power of unconditional love, persistence, and determination.

My brother Mark taught me the power of faith and family when he selflessly left his family for a week and flew to Victoria to be by my side and support me in my darkest moment. He continued to support me when I could not support myself, and for that I thank him. Despite our differences in faith, he was there for me, as was my whole family and close friends.

Jodie taught me the power of never, ever giving up, even when it feels like there's no hope. She continued to support and encourage me to keep going when I didn't know if I could.

During this time a good friend of mine, Nigel, lost almost his entire family in a car accident. Life changed for him in seconds. This made me appreciate the life I did have and how I needed to find the strength to carry on. Nigel taught me the power of living in the moment and appreciating every second, because you just don't know when life can change. It can happen in a heartbeat.

My friend Amy helped me see belief in all of the tools I had at my disposal. I started with Louise Hay's forgiveness meditation. I knew I needed to forgive myself. I was living with such intense guilt over the separation, my financial situation, failing in my work environment, and not being a parent to Dylan. I felt like a complete failure and lost all self-belief. Once I did the forgiveness meditation for several days, things started to shift. Amy taught me the power of sharing your personal journey. Through sharing her journey, she helped me survive and get through the other side.

My parents helped me out financially, and it relieved a lot of stress. Then I was awarded workcover, which I had resisted for such a long time. I started doing hypnosis every day for stress management, listened in on the NeuroSummit, and put a heap of tools to the test on myself. I became my own best client. A number of really good friends taught me the power of true friendship and compassion when they were there for me during my time of darkness.

I'm now back at work in a new role of Wellbeing Officer for Alternate Programs. This role entails working with our most complex students with significant issues and trauma. I love it, and I bring a completely different perspective and experience to it, because of my own life's journey. I understand post-traumatic stress, anxiety, depression, and trauma and can offer a whole new level of understanding to our students.

My line manager and the education system taught me the strength of being empowered in situations and systems that dis-empower you.

I'm now focused back on my business, Haven Heart Healing, and have a clear path ahead of me. I believe that sometimes life has to fall apart in order to rebuild the new, and this is what happened to me.

I recently met Ray who taught me the power of self love and self-acceptance, as well as complete trust. I've always found it hard to trust in myself and others or that everything happens for a reason. I've often felt the need to control my life, but when I experienced my crash where I felt like I had no control over anything, I found the power in surrender and letting go.

CHAPTER 12: Kelly Fletcher

Haven Heart Healing

Throughout her career, Kelly Fletcher has always had a passion for growing and learning. As a result, she went on to study and become qualified in a range of modalities.

Kelly started her own business, Haven Heart Healing, in 2014 where she uses her skills to assist others to get where they want to be in life. Kelly loves inspiring people to overcome the fears and obstacles that are holding them back, so they can create the life of their dreams.

Kelly brings to her clients her own life experience of being at the depths of despair to a position of self-empowerment. Kelly is also a Louise Hay workshop leader and Life Coach and enjoys teaching people how to truly love themselves in order to change their life.

To access Kelly's one-on-one coaching and workshops, please connect with her on Facebook at Haven Heart Healing:

https://www.facebook.com/Haven-Heart-Healing-584898301545012/timeline/

You can also email her at kf_fletcher@bigpond.com or phone her at 0407000955 for a free half-hour discovery session to discover how Kelly can assist you in transforming your life and overcoming your current obstacles.

CHAPTER 13

Therese Howell

> *"Never bend your head. Always hold it high. Look the world straight in the eye."*

Helen Keller

CHAPTER 13: Therese Howell

CHAPTER THIRTEEN
Therese Howell

Therese has more than ten years of experience in grant making and eight years of experience in charitable program funding management. She's passionate about effective philanthropy.

The first time I met Therese was when we were seated at the same table at the Duke of Edinburgh Gala Dinner in Melbourne. She's an inspiration. She reminds me of what Mother Teresa said. "It's not how much you do but how much love you put in the actions that you do." Therese puts a lot of love into her work, be it facilitating at a camp, helping a not-for-profit organisation secure funding, or just being a wonderful friend with a listening ear.

Tell me about your early life.

I was born and raised on dairy farms in country NSW and Victoria. My parents were farmers in Bega, East Gippsland, and the Latrobe Valley. When I was eighteen, during Year 12 of my schooling, I moved out. It's typical in the country to leave home at a young age. I took a lot of classes, because I loved learning. I used to clean motel rooms in the morning before school. Then I would go to school, and in the afternoon during the week I did two TAFE courses. One was hospitality, and the other was photography.

On Friday and Saturday nights I worked tending bar in a bistro, and on Sundays I worked in a nursing home. You know, I always said I never wanted to waste my parents' money, and if I needed to go to university to have a certain career, then I would do it when I discovered what the career was.

Hospitality was outside of nine to five and a great transitional industry, especially if it goes toward your studies, but long-term you have no social life. So I would say to go and get your life experience and overcome your limitations.

What did you finally decide to do?

Work in the country was scarce. I did a traineeship in administration, so I wound up doing administrative work, while my partner and future husband, Rob, was a carpenter. He had a lot of work in the city, so he'd stay in backpacker's places in Melbourne during the week, and then came home on weekends.

After six months, my work had dried up. The company I'd been working for lost a lot of contracts. There was lots of work in Melbourne, so we took a leap of faith, and I networked through my friends to let them know I was looking for work. I got a role at State Trustees as an administrative assistant, the very bottom of the tree. I knew nothing about the business when I first started. Here I was this little girl in the big city. My first interview was the first time I caught a train, and the first time I'd been in a lift above two floors. I was proud of myself for being fierce by taking risks and confronting new experiences head on.

I really fell in love with State Trustees. Through them I was introduced to a lot of different financial mechanisms of giving. I know that sounds strange from what people know of State Trustees, but I worked in the nursing home team, so I would look after people by paying their bills, because they didn't have the mental capacity to look after themselves.

That was one of my many different roles. I also worked in the Testamentary Trust division. That meant I looked after trust funds for children under the age of eighteen who had a parent or grandparent who'd passed away and left money in trust to them. I was responsible for making decisions about their finances. I loved the diversity of it and caring for people.

After growing up in a rural community that cared and supported each other, it was a fundamental part of my being to help people. Now here I was being paid to care about people. I guess that willingness to learn and being open served me well. I quickly became well known within the organisation. There was probably a staff of about four hundred, but I had a habit of not being afraid to introduce myself, and I shook hands like my dad always taught me to. He said when you meet someone to look the person in the eye, give a firm and confident handshake, and think of yourself as their equal. You show respect, and respect is returned.

CHAPTER 13: Therese Howell

I think I got a name for myself as the country bumpkin. When I first started working and living in Melbourne, instead of the picture of my family on my desk I had a photograph of my parents' farm. Everyone would ask about the picture, and I'd say I needed to see something green. But I was also known as someone who could get things done and think outside of the box. Sometimes things needed to happen, and they didn't always fit into a nice little neat box on a form. Over time I changed a lot of forms they're using to this day.

I eventually held the role of Charitable Trust Consultant, and I managed a portfolio of more than one-hundred-forty trusts at a value of over forty-eight million. In that role I was thrust into the world of assessing charities. I ran grants, programs, and applications. Charities told me about their projects, and why they should get money. It opened up a whole new world for me.

This job must have presented a lot of challenges. How did you deal with them?

I felt a lot of pressure, because so many charities felt they were deserving of the money more than others. I had to take a lot of factors into consideration. I was also committed to doing the role justice. What I wound up doing was implementing grants panels where we brought in leaders from the disability and environment world and asked their advice. Getting a more qualified opinion helped me to do my job properly. Sometimes the simplest solution is the best.

I don't like red tape, because I do question authority, and these people do not like to be questioned. That didn't stop me. I'm not one for sitting on my hands or not saying how it is. I was introduced to some wonderful charities and projects, and I wanted to get out of the office to see what they were doing. To make sure everything was done properly. You know, it's interesting how the little intercepts on our journey eventually take us to our goals.

What were some of the projects?

One of the projects was funding for groups that needed a bus to transport kids to a disability playground called Hays Paddock. I was intrigued by this Hays Paddock and why it was so much more special than their local park. I happened to be renting nearby and went to check it out. It was quite profound. The entrance has a sign that tells the story about a community getting together to create a playground where the elements had been designed so children of all different abilities could participate and play together. It made sense to me. I was enthralled by the vision of a community working together to enable ability for those with disabilities. I was in wonder of the tenacity of these children's families. So fast track two years later when I had my first child, Jack, who was born missing his hand, and lo and behold, I'm thrust into the world of disability.

How did that change your life, and how did your experience come into play?

I'd worked in this industry caring for people, and I worked with charities and gotten to know the tax laws, the requirements, the programs, what works, and what doesn't. I had all of this wealth of knowledge, and yet here I was just floundering around not knowing what to do. No longer could I put something in my calendar and let it happen. You know, when this baby cried I had to drop everything. It changed my entire lifestyle. I'd always had a lot of control in my life. I'm an organisational person. I kind of naively believed bad things only happened to bad people. That perhaps smoking or drinking during pregnancy resulted in a disability. After Jack was born, those beliefs were shattered. It broke the way I thought about everything. I could no longer look at situations in specific categories.

Up until that point, I'd had the white-picket lifestyle. I met my husband when I was sixteen, we got married when I was twenty two, and we bought our first house when I was twenty four. From there I was supposed to have the perfect 2.2 children at the age of twenty seven. Everything was all lined up in a row. Then everything broke. It all came undone. I had to revaluate myself. I was going to be the mother of a child with a disability. I didn't even know whether I'd be a good mother or not, or if I'd be able to handle the challenges ahead. I'm lucky I have a wonderful husband who's centred and completely accepting. He basically said, "It is what it is. We'll work it out." My husband is a *She'll be right, mate* kind of guy. We're the perfect opposites, so we complement each other. I'm structure, while he's flexible.

I'm the eldest of five children, so I was the surrogate mother from the age of ten. I cooked for the family and did the housework while my mum was in the dairy. I was happy to take on the role. I was always wired that way. I was always solid. You could rely on me to get things done. I had to give the other kids their chores on the farm and make sure they did their tasks, while I often did the cooking, the washing, and the housework.

CHAPTER 13: Therese Howell

So this solid, reliable person, the one who'd always helped everybody else, was broken and unsure of herself. There was a fear, because how would people perceive me from that moment forward if they saw how broken I was? Would they still trust me, look to me to help them, to be a support for them? Because that's fundamentally a part of who I am. I've always been a giver. I wound up wearing this mask, even to my husband and my mum. I didn't want them to worry about me. I thought if I showed how broken I felt and how lacking in confidence I was, and how shattered I was, it would affect how they saw me in the future. There was a fear of really letting anyone into my emotions at that time.

I was lucky there was a lovely lady at State Trustees who must have seen something in my eyes. I could tell she just knew. She told me the company had an anonymous counselling program. My first thought was that I was raised on the farm, so what did I need a counsellor for? You get in there like a man, and you get a job done.

But I knew it was for my own good and relented. I wound up with a fantastic counsellor. This lady just kind of got me from day one. It was like the biggest weight off my shoulders, because I was starting to have suicidal thoughts. I know I wasn't really going to do anything, but these thoughts would flit through from time to time. Once when we were out in the bush and travelling on a cliff face, I remember thinking I could just take a step, and I'd be gone. Or I'd just drop off that bridge. I'd never, ever in my life had thoughts like that. They were intermittent, but it still surprised me.

I struggled to get my head around being a mum of a kid with disabilities. I just did not want to be *that* person in *that* box. The counsellor said it was my brain thinking of backup plans as to how I could get out of the situation. She told me to go out into the paddock and yell and scream, "THIS SUCKS! I HATE THIS! WHY ME?" She said I was entitled to do this, and then get over it. To have my moment, have my cry, be angry, be annoyed, be frustrated. She said my life was going to change, but that it wasn't necessarily a bad thing.

Fast track ten years, and my Lord, I wouldn't give my son back for the world. He's amazing. He's given me so much. He showed me everyone and everything has the right to be unique and expressive and flowing and flexible as it needs to. He's given me the ability to think beyond limitations and to aspire to set great goals and not be limited. Those are huge qualities. To think that they're given to me by my own son is fundamental.

The journey of parenthood turned out not to be this scary, horrible place I'd imagined when I was pregnant but this amazing journey of growth and development and pride. In the world of disability, careers, and business success, it all comes back to sharing and seeking knowledge, new learning, new experiences, and new adventures. That is fundamental to our growth and success.

When Jack was one, I figured I had this parenting gig under control. After all, I'd managed to keep him alive for an entire year. Life was starting to take shape again. I guess all of my fears hadn't transpired. From his birth, to be honest, I'd had a sense of shame. When I first met my son I kind of said, "Wow, you're not just a baby without a hand. You're a whole person. Look at those eyes, look at that hair, and look at that cute little chin. There was so much more to him than just the hand. Even as his mother, until I had that baby in my arms, I hadn't made that revelation or come to that understanding.

As I got my head out of the nappies and lack of sleep and had some more transparency in my world, I started to worry if he'd hit his milestones. Is he going to crawl? How's he going to ride a bike? How's he going to feed himself? How's he going to hold a bottle? Are these things even possible? Should I be encouraging him to have tummy time and crawl, if it's just not possible? I had all of these questions, these doubts, and I thought, you know, surely he's not the only kid who has one hand. There has to be others out there.

Then I wondered where all of the others were. I searched for groups. I questioned so many people who didn't have the answers I needed. I would go from one dead end to another, to another. Then I'd get vague information like, "Oh, I heard there's a clinic at the Royal Children's that maybe deals with kids like yours." I'd ask all of these questions and find these loose connections. It took a long time and perseverance. If I'd stopped at the first road block, I would still be in no-man's land. I really had to push.

At last I found the limb deficiency clinic at the Royal Children's Hospital, and the only group they were aware of was in Queensland. I sought out some other parents and families. In the limb clinic, I put up notices of group get-togethers and spoke to special playgroups, maternal child health nurses, and families.

CHAPTER 13: Therese Howell

Did you ever think of starting your own charity?

Due to my background, I was aware of all of the red tape involved in starting my own charity, and I knew that wasn't an avenue I wanted to explore. I didn't need money. I just needed to connect with other families in order to get some support and share knowledge. I didn't want to reinvent the wheel. To me it was simple. It was just get-togethers at a coffee place or parks and playgrounds. That's how it started. Then when Jack turned eight, and I had two-hundred families connected, we ran surf days and golf days and Christmas parties with a one-legged Santa. I was connecting. There were adult groups, as well as groups that were specific to hands only. When I found those families, older children that were like my son, I had role models. I was like "Oh, yeah, you're so having tummy time, because you can crawl. You can."

It made you gain more confidence.

I did get more confidence in my parenting. My husband as well. I distinctly remember a shift in parenting one day when my husband was on the roof fixing tiles. He's a carpenter, so being a tradie and up on ladders is nothing. My not-quite two-year-old baby boy in nappies started climbing the ladder. I'm having kittens watching this.

Rob was at the edge, when he had a look down and said, "Shh. He will know when it's too high. Trust him." My heart was hammering, and all I could think was that I was going to kill my husband if anything happened to Jack. You know, forget that Jack's missing one hand climbing up the ladder. He's also under the age of two. When he got to the fourth rung, about a metre off the ground, he looked up at Rob then back down, and made his way back. He took his time and felt his way. I got the camera out, and I actually have a photo of this glorious, nappy baby climbing down a ladder.

When he reached the bottom, my husband said, "We've got to let him go. We've got to let him learn. We've got to let him know his own body. We've got to trust him. We've got to let him have experiences. He will hurt himself. He will make mistakes, but that's how he'll learn." My wise husband.

From that moment it was a combination of what my husband said, as well as having a health nurse tell me that children learn what's called auto actions before the age of five. When we have a drink, we don't think *open my hand, close my hand, and lift it to my mouth.* We just do it. Almost everything you learn before the age of five often becomes auto actions. So basically the nurse said to let him learn.

Then we had this child who was tying his shoelaces and riding his bike before his peers were able to. He climbed Ayres Rock at age five. There are photos of him holding onto the chain and looking at the car park. These are the building blocks of parenthood. We're building this little boy. Jack is now eleven, and he can do everything on his own. All of our limiting beliefs were taken away.

I went back to work part-time at State Trustees when Jack was one year old, while I still created support networks in Victoria from my home computer. As I got connected with more families, I became quickly aware that limb difference congenitally is random. This gave me the confidence to have my second child Alyssa, born three years after Jack and with no disabilities.

You had two children and a fulltime job. How did you manage it all?

With two children, working in the city, and living on the fringe of Melbourne, the travel was killing me. It was nearly three hours of my day I was sitting on a train or a tram that I was missing out on time with my children. I wound up taking a local job closer to home with the City of Casey, distributing grants to the local community, and I loved it.

Being a country girl and loving nature so much, it must be hard for you to live in the suburbs.

Suburban living is a struggle sometimes. My mum had five children, and I jokingly told her that if she'd lived in suburbia, she would have been hauled off to DSS every second day for screaming at her children.

I grew up predominately on the Snowy River in Orbost. We would fish from our veranda and swim in the river in all seasons. We had a boat, and we would go digging for mud crabs and sand worms. We lived off the land with fruit trees and vegetable gardens and chickens and cows, surrounded by the beauty of nature. The silence was beautiful. I feel sorry for those who've never gone on a walk and been totally alone like in a back paddock or out on the land. To have total silence, total freedom of thought. The ability to sing or scream at the top of your lungs without anyone hearing you.

CHAPTER 13: Therese Howell

I've always been a country girl, and my husband loves four wheel drives and camping, so after I worked at the City of Casey for a while, the whole family wanted to get back to nature. We took some long service leave and travelled for eight months around Australia. We went through South Australia and Adelaide and did a quick flick up to Lake Eyre through Cooper Pedy, then back down along the Nullarbor, over to Western Australia, through the bottom of WA, up through Perth, over to Rottnest, out through The Pilbara, up to Broome, and the beautiful Cape Leveque, which is one of my favourite models of modern Aboriginal community living. It's a beautiful blend of culture and modern employment. I love that the park rangers in Cape Leveque are Aboriginal. They're the caretakers of the land. It's such a natural employability, and they're good at border patrol, because they don't want any more boats.

I'm highly interested in Aboriginal projects and in indigenous programs because of my level of understanding and a respect for the Aboriginal community in paving the way forward. I believe in the Aboriginal community, and I believe in empowerment for those communities. They're all so special. I've given that to my children as well. My husband and I believe in living in the moment. If you want to do something, don't pigeonhole yourself and plan on doing it in twenty years when you retire. What if retirement never comes?

My son was five at the time, and my youngest, Alyssa, was two years old. Changing nappies in the red dust was a challenge, but it was so worth it, because we'd saved up so we didn't have to work. We just had to enjoy our time together and have our adventures. If we were all feeling a little bit under the weather, we'd find a nice spot with a pool and relax, refresh, and gear up for the next challenge.

We were often the only family in caravan parks in the top end, because you have to remember most other children were back at school. We were totally surrounded by grey nomads, and consistently they would come and congratulate us and say they wished they could be us, because they were in a caravan and couldn't go off-road.

We saw some of the most beautiful places. One time we had to hike for two hours on a rocky, untended path to get to this waterfall. Everyone thinks you can just retire to travel around Australia and see everything when you're eighty. We saw so many retired people in tears. One gentleman fell and broke his hip and had to be airlifted out. He was crushed. He'd waited his entire life to do this. It was heartbreaking. We wanted to have these experiences while we had our health, and it was brought home when we saw what would have happened if we'd waited.

Not everyone is a camper, so I often tell people that if they only do one trip with their children, to go to Alice Springs and Ayers Rock, because you can do the centre on any budget or go five star if that's your thing. Or you can go bush camping crazy like we did.

What did these experiences teach you?

Now when I do grants, funding, charities, and philanthropy, I have a deeper understanding of some of the remote challenges that come with the problem-solving in these regions. The unique challenges within each environment. You can't paint each problem with the same brush. Seeing everything firsthand gave me a deeper knowledge, a deeper understanding, when it comes to grant giving and grant making. All of these incidents build into a life experience. They've driven my passion to take my knowledge and help someone who needed support and to connect with people.

I also wanted to be a part of the solution to my problem. There's all of these little life experiences that have all come together to help me move forward. I realised I had this model of supporting people. I also saw I was becoming the epicentre. Everything and everyone was dependent on me.

Part of that revelation came about because at the age of thirty four, I was diagnosed with thyroid cancer. I knew that if something did happen to me, where would all of this knowledge go? It helped make me reflect on the families that were now connected through their children with limb difference, and that I had a duty to not be the epicentre. I needed to empower others to take on the work, to help each other.

I had to give a home to this beautiful support network I'd created. I moved it to a charitable organisation that was working with adults with limb difference. What it meant was this charity could now be holistic from birth through death. It could be a support charity for those with limb loss. It was an opportunity to combine the two networks under the one charity. It made sense. It allowed me

CHAPTER 13: Therese Howell

to bring my network under one umbrella with more opportunities for funding, and other volunteers that could share the load.

I was nominated for a Vodafone World of Difference award by the charity. After a competitive interview process and online voting, I was one of five participants selected. The award provided wages for one year and additional project funds to establish a national children and youth support service that would serve as a legacy for future generations to move forward.

In that year I was the first non-medical presenter at the international prosthetics and orthotics conference. It was quite an honour. It involved talking to the hospitals. A lot of them worked in isolation. They didn't know what each of them was doing. I helped give them the knowledge to bring them together. It was a wonderful year and a great program to help develop.

It sounds like you had quite a busy schedule. How were you able to find balance?

At the end of that time I think I'd done twelve interstate trips. My youngest was just starting school, and I kind of flopped onto the coach. After doing the year of developing and bringing that program to life, I was exhausted. I was determined to be more present for my family and to find a better balance between work and family. I didn't have my children so that someone else could raise them.

After a crazy year of trying to balance work and motherhood, I came to a critical moment that explains where my path led me. A big fat dose of mother's guilt made me entertain the idea of working from home as a consultant. After completing a large, fulltime project, I felt my relationship and quality time with my children were suffering. I realised I was in a unique position with my experience in grant making, grant seeking, program development, and as a charity beneficiary. This is a niche area. The knowledge, experience and skill set I have are unique. I understood all of the elements of philanthropy from all the different variables. As a consultant, I could have a broader impact.

It gave me the best of both worlds, because I would still have flexibility. So now I'll block out my calendar for the children's athletics carnival and let my clients know I'm sorry, but I have other commitments. I've learned to balance my life. Now that mother's guilt is a lot lower. I'm still doing grant writing and some grant seeking, and those do have a deadline. In my industry, a deadline is a deadline, because otherwise, you have to wait another twelve months. It's a good thing my parents still have a farm, so I try to give my kids at least four or five days during school holidays to go up there. My parents love that time with the kids. If I can just get a solid couple of days of working without distractions, I can be free for the reminder of the holidays. That way I'm totally present and not kind of flitting off to do this or that and coming back distracted. I'm totally all there.

What kind of clients do you work with?

I'm so fortunate that some of my clients include wildlife and conservation, as well as scientific research in regard to post-natal and peri-natal depression. Some of my clients work in the disability field in support and community giving. Most of them are charities. As a not for profit, you could be incorporated, but you may not have what's known as DGR, which is deductible gift recipient. Without that DGR status, a lot of philanthropic grants are not open to you.

I just assisted my client to get more than three million in funding. One of those projects was winning a Google Global Impact challenge grant. I'm helping to revive funding and seek grant assistance for these amazing projects that are changing the world. For instance, the Google grant is to fund a technology that's going to change the way we clean oil spills.

Another project is the development of an online intervention, the first of its kind, for peri-natal depression. One of the biggest barriers of antenatal and postnatal depression is in intervention. This project is quite personal to me, because it's something I've experienced. It's self-regulated, and we can move ourselves beyond, but some of us need assistance. The problem is that it's still such a taboo to seek that assistance. Helping charities to do these projects is my way of being the string that brings these to fruition. I'm getting the funds so these projects can happen. It's a wonderful, wonderful role. I get to be a mum, and I get to change the world.

I'm also the executive officer of the Casey-Cardinia Foundation that works within the Casey Cardinia community, local charities, and not for profits, to help change and make a difference in the local community. It means I get to share my skills with a broad variety of people rather than streamlined in one area.

CHAPTER 13: Therese Howell

I do workshops with local government. They call me in to run workshops for them, and they invite their local not-for-profit organizations. I teach the fundamentals of applying for grants and give them some skills and knowledge to help them be more self sustaining, like writing their own grant applications and seeking funds. I help the little guys. The big guys usually have their own grant resources.

I have clients on my waiting list, so there's a possibility that in the future I'll have to train others or take on an admin. I've had to learn how to say no. It's difficult. I look at the different projects, and then decide which are the most worthy. I don't care whether it's work or not. If a charity has a program I don't believe in or I disagree with or I can't see the value in, I speak up. Years ago, I never would have done that. Where it goes from here is exciting, and I'm sure I'm making lots of mistakes, but I look forward to the mistakes, because I can learn from them. Our futures are never determinable, and I may decide to go back to a regular job, but for now, I love helping people.

You've won other awards for the work you do.

In 2012 I received an Australia Day Citizen of the Year award for my volunteer work with limb different children and in the community. It was such a wonderful honour. I met all of the other potential recipients, and we were all told to write a speech. Because I'd worked at City of Casey I have a great relationship with them, as well as my local government. I sit on their access and inclusion committee and volunteer on other projects. At the pre-dinner I was speaking with the mayor, and he asked how my speech was coming along. I jokingly asked, "Have you met the other potential recipients? I don't need to write a speech. The other candidates are amazing, and they have it in the bag." He kind of called me over to the side and stressed how important it was for me to consider writing that speech. I figured it meant I'd be getting some notable mention or something. It still didn't sink in I might win.

I had this light-hearted attempt at writing some sort of a speech. When I went up, I didn't call out the mayor, but I did kind of say I was nudged to write the speech, and I still didn't believe I'd won. In true me fashion, I did the entire speech without looking at a word I had written. I still don't know why I wrote one. I often just speak off the cuff.

I knew I'd won the award for helping myself and others. I do what I do, because I love doing it. I didn't learn anything new or all of a sudden become a doctor to solve that problem. It was hard for me to understand why I'd won the award. But from what I'm told it's because I could have just sat back and been the beneficiary or a victim and had myself a pity party or waited for people to bring me what I needed. Instead, if I didn't have what I needed, I went and got it. That was the mother in me. And I'm now the mother of all of these children with limb difference.

What does it mean to you to be a fierce and fabulous woman?

Like a good mum, I'm not scared to smack people on the bottom and correct their behaviours. Some of that feminine force comes from an earthy upbringing on the farm and the rural environment. I learned how to overcome problems. You're talking about a large family. Seven people in a three-bedroom home on a farm, working seven days a week, twenty-four hours a day. Hard work for very little money. We didn't do after-school activities. There was no way my parents could have afforded that.

It all comes back to a quick story. One day I was riding in the car with my children, and Alyssa said that when Jack would go to pick up her up from her classroom, her friend would run away because of his "freaky hand." In my head I was wondering how I was going to deal with this, when Jack, who was nine at the time, said, "It's okay, Mum. When I go pick up Alyssa next week, I'll just take her friend quietly to the home corner away from the other kids, so she's not embarrassed, and I'll just show her my hand. I'll let her touch it and feel it, and I'll show her that it's just a little hand, and it's not freaky. I'll make sure she's feeling okay."

So there were two things in that statement I instantly took away while I was crying and trying not to let him see me. One, he saw the problem as Alyssa's friend's and not his. He totally didn't take it onto himself. But two, he saw how he could be the solution to that problem by taking away the fear, so this little girl could be comfortable with him. Now Alyssa's friend adores him so much, she's like a puppy dog. In that moment I congratulated myself. I could retire. He's been parented well. Job done.

That transfers over to the business world. As fierce and fabulous women, we have the ability to grow our building blocks of self confidence, keep adding to

CHAPTER 13: Therese Howell

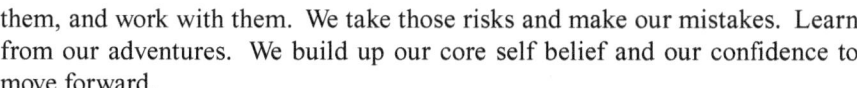

them, and work with them. We take those risks and make our mistakes. Learn from our adventures. We build up our core self belief and our confidence to move forward.

What have you had to give up to do what you do?

One is financial certainty. My husband is self-employed as a carpenter, so his income is erratic. It was always nice that I had a regular job with a regular income. It came in every week, solid as a rock. For a control freak like I am, to give up that financial certainty was difficult. I had to give up control and routine, because in my world, like I said before, a deadline is a deadline is a deadline.

Mostly I work from home, but going into my clients' offices helps keep the connection and communication flowing. I also feel that if they see me working, they know I'm doing something. There's a visual element. I'm still not totally working from home, but this system works for me. Sometimes to be able to go to my children's activities or pick them up from school, I'll have to go back and make up the lost hours at another time. That means I've had to give up that nine-to-five routine of going to the same place, the same train, and the same bus every day. My schedule is all over the place.

This is sometimes hard on my husband. His hours are kind of set, so he doesn't always understand why I'm working so late. I've had to speak with him and get the balance right there. But as I said, he's the yin to my yang. He's good at sometimes letting me know I'm doing something wrong if for five nights in a row I've worked until midnight. He knows what a strain it can be on me.

I also had to give up camaraderie. Because I'm working from home by myself, I don't have a team any more. I don't have work colleagues to go and have a coffee with or lunch with to whinge about my boss. I always tell myself I have a terrible boss. She's terrible. I can only complain about myself. This is extra difficult, because I'm a talker. I love a good chat. It's one of my greatest assets and one of my greatest faults. It's strange when I get around someone who's not much of a talker. I apologize and explain to them it's a by-product of working from home. I'm a brain-stormer. My poor mom. She lives in the country, so I had to get an unlimited plan, because the bills were getting expensive.

On the flipside, what have you gained?

Flexibility. I've always been so rigid and controlled. I've started to become more fluid, which is nice. I do have a bit more of a backbone as well and take the day off when I need to. My son deserves to have me watch him swim at the swimming carnival. That's why I work from home. My kids are priority number one. But there are times when I've had to apologize and tell them they have to go to after-school care two or three times that week, because I need to get a million-dollar grant for a client, and if I don't make it happen, I'm kind of in big trouble.

I've gained a good work ethic. I've been more experiential in looking at different opportunities and following those opportunities. I've gained a deeper self confidence and made little decisions where I pat myself on the back. You know, one of my rules in business is that I never submit a grant application until I have manager approval. That means it rests on them and not me. I'm not pressing the button until they say it's approved. I need to protect me. I've definitely gained a deeper belief in trusting my gut feeling.

My family and friends live in the country, and to them my work is this big mystery. How do I explain what I do? When someone asks, I say I work in philanthropy, grants, funding, and charities. It's led to some really weird conversations. I come from quite a simple, rural background. I haven't gone to university. I've never studied. All my learning has been on the job. I've done a few TAFE courses that I needed here and there and got a certificate in business. When I worked with the State Trustees, I did get a trustee certification. I was the first charitable trust consultant ever employed who didn't have university qualifications. It's because at that time I was known for getting the job done and being a problem solver, as well as a communicator. I was able to work within teams.

How is your health after the cancer scare?

This year I'm five years cancer-free, which is wonderful. I guess I come from a family that has a high providence of it. I'm screened every year for breast and ovarian cancer, which goes hand in hand with my thyroid. My grandmother died at the age of forty two. In three years I'll be the same age, so I try to keep on top of it. My mum has already had breast cancer in her late forties. You have

CHAPTER 13: Therese Howell

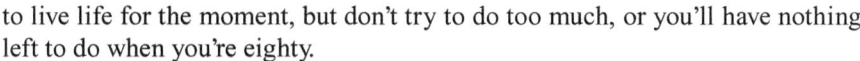

to live life for the moment, but don't try to do too much, or you'll have nothing left to do when you're eighty.

Are you still travelling?

Yes. When we travel, we always enjoy it like we'll never get back but also leave something unseen, so that if we do get to go back, we'll have something new to discover. When we travel, I write a blog. Family and friends loved it, and I have fun taking photos, so those photography courses came in handy. Everyone suggested I write a book or put it in a magazine. I figured I'm already doing all of the work, so why not? Then I asked myself why somebody would want to read about my travels. Is this information valuable to somebody?

I went out on a limb and rang a few magazines that contained articles about people who travelled. This began five years of being a freelance writer and photographer for Bauer Media. I did stories for *Camper Trailer Australia* and *Caravan World* magazine. I didn't go into it like all of a sudden I was a freelance writer or photographer but more as a hobby. I'm doing it when I have the time and on my terms. It's money for jam. I don't have any skills, I just happen to write. I don't even know how to use my camera. I point and shoot. But you know, I'm willing to have a go, and I'm willing to try.

Along with everything else, you still volunteer.

I've been fortunate that along the way I've picked up other volunteer roles. I'm always busy with my hand in lots of different pots. At the moment I'm volunteering with Amp Camp, a national annual camp for teenagers with limb loss and limb difference, as well as Livvi's Place, a playground for children of all abilities, only the second of its kind in Victoria and similar to the Hays Paddock I came across back in my days as a consultant with State Trustees.

When it comes to Amp Camp and Livvi's Place disability playground, I volunteer because I have a passion and an understanding of the project. It's not so altruistic. I'm not going out there thinking I want to do some good deed. Good finds me, and I'm not scared to say no. I shouldn't be doing something if I don't understand it, but I'm not scared to say yes when I'm the right person. It's a bit like when I went looking for the support of other parents. There are critical moments. One of my other critical moments was when I realized my child was old enough that I could pass on the information I'd gathered. Right now there's a mum who's just been told her baby is not going to have a hand or a foot. I know what that feels like and where some of the information is. I then wondered how I could help these people.

I had to dig deep within myself, and there was a moment when I realised I had these admin skills. I could write emails. I know how to connect with people. How to write information that's engaging and sensitive and appropriate and professional. So why wasn't I doing it? I guess it's that I'm not afraid to look at myself and wonder if I could be a solution to a problem. With the Livvi's Place project, I came across the charity Touched by Olivia Foundation that was building playgrounds like Hays Paddock. It gave me knowledge as to the value of that project. I could talk about why we needed it, because I'm active in the community.

Just in my playgroup alone we had my son Jack and two boys with autism, as well as one young man in a wheelchair who had no verbal skills. There's no way you could get that wheelchair into a regular playground. As for the kids with autism, if it's not fully fenced, forget it. They're escapees, and they'll be on the road in two seconds flat. Mum is sitting on tenterhooks. So knowing that experience, and then seeing a solution to that problem, how could I not say yes to helping with a project that could make such a difference?

What advice do you have for those who don't feel they have the qualifications to pursue their dreams?

When people have circumstances they think will prohibit or limit them, I think it comes back to that core messaging. Think beyond your limitations. Strive. As young kids today embark on careers, I would tell them to go and get experience. Don't be scared. Work and be active. Volunteer your time to learn. If you want it bad enough and strive toward it, there are no limitations.

Some questions I think everyone should ask themselves are: "What skills do I have?" "What piece of the puzzle am I in the tapestry of life?" "Where is my fit?" "Where is my ability to contribute, and why am I not doing that?" Young women need to be themselves. What's the worst that can happen if you fail? Is it really that bad? What's holding you back from trying? Because it's nothing to give of your skills, your passion, your knowledge. It's so easy.

CHAPTER 13: Therese Howell

Do you have any quotes you'd like to share?

I have a list of them:

- If you don't imagine, nothing ever happens at all. – John Green

- Forever is such a long time. – Jack Howell, Age 11, born with a left hand limb deficiency.

- There are no excuses – Caitlin Wilson, 19, born with a left hand limb deficiency.

- It is what you do that determines who you are. – Matthew Yates, 19, born with an ongoing fragile bone condition that limits activity and has resulted in amputation.

- I am LIMBitless – Caitlin Wilson, 19, born with a left hand limb deficiency.

- If you can't win, make the person in front break the record. – Don Elgin, congenital below-knee amputee, motivational speaker, and three-time Paralympian.

- I am perfectly imperfect. – Caitlin Wilson, 19, born with a left hand limb deficiency.

- There is no such thing as normal. – Dwayne Fernandes, congenital double leg amputee and record-breaking, tall building stair runner.

- A rose without a petal is still a rose. – Sami Hanrahan, arm amputee.

- No matter the outcome, there is never any failure if you have done your absolute best. – Kathleen O'Kelly-Kennedy, congenital below knee amputee.

- I am not what has happened to me, I am what I choose to become. – C G Jung

- When life gets you down, do you wanna know what you've gotta do? Just keep swimming. Just keep swimming. Just keep swimming, swimming, swimming. – Dory, *Finding Nemo*

Fierce & Fabulous ~ The Feminine Force of Success

Therese Howell
GRANTS AND FUNDING CONSULTANT

MAKING A DIFFERENCE

Therese provides services to both grant seekers and grant makers. Her extensive experience in philanthropic and government grantmaking, combined with charitable program development, provides a unique philanthropic perspective.

As an Australia Day Citizen of the Year and World of Difference Winner, Therese is passionate about innovative projects that make a real difference and have a lasting impact in the community.

A REAL AND LASTING IMPACT WITHIN AUSTRALIAN COMMUNITIES

Therese is a well-established grants and funding consultant with more than fifteen years of experience. She's built a career around helping charities and not-for-profit organisations achieve their goals to help others.

From supporting wildlife organizations, to conservation, disability, perinatal depression, cancer, youth disadvantage, and community charitable projects, Therese secures an average of two million dollars in funding each year to support Australian charities in making a real and lasting impact in the community.

EFFECTIVE PHILANTHROPY

For the majority of Therese's working career, she has been immersed in grant distribution to charities through trusts, foundations, and government. As a consultant, she is determined to inspire philanthropic organisations to deliver grants with a focus on effective philanthropy and making a difference. Through her work with local government, Therese provides grant and funding workshops to small community groups. She teaches them the skills to appropriately seek grants and sustainable funding options.

"Philanthropy is more than just giving. Why put a pebble in a pond, when you could put a rock in a puddle?"

INTEGRITY AND HEART

Therese is one of Australia's leading Grants and Funding Consultants, with notable success in high-profile grants such as the Google Global Impact Challenge grant. She works honestly with clients to identify opportunities and barriers, while finding solutions to enable change. In her effort to lead by example, she has volunteered and been the driving force behind the establishment of a number of Australian charitable projects, including AMP CAMP, Australia's only camp for amputee youth, Livvi's Place, the first all-ability playground in South East Victoria, and the Children and Youth Limb difference support service.

Therese Howell ~ 0439905533 ~ rthowell@netspace.net.au ~ Web: theresehowell.strikingly.com

CHAPTER 14

Rebecca McIntyre

"When you make women millionaires, you change the world."

Petter Morck

CHAPTER 14: Rebecca McIntyre

CHAPTER FOURTEEN
Rebecca McIntyre

Rebecca is a National Vice President of an International company and embodies what it means to be a successful businessperson. Throughout her life, she's made major sacrifices while focussing on the long term. She had a crystal-clear Why for success and stayed committed to it. The result: Rebecca has improved many lives, including her own, and now she's there full time for her family

I wanted to give a special mention to Rebecca who has contributed so much to making Fierce & Fabulous *a reality. Here is her short story about how she wound up living her dream.*

I've lived in a country town with about eighteen thousand people my whole life. I always knew I would be destined for something big, but I didn't know what that would look like for me. As I grew up in the schooling system, I soon realised it was not to be found in formal education.

I had a spirit to help and motivate others that I now know was the entrepreneur inside of me. But I really never knew what I wanted to do with my life. That is, until one day I was offered to take a peek into network marketing. I was not expecting my destiny to be wrapped up in this opportunity, especially considering it was in health and wellness, and I have no experience in that industry. But what I did have was a passion to motivate, help, and inspire others. I had the need to show people they could do whatever they wanted if they put their mind to it, and it didn't matter where they lived or where they were from. I developed a whole new lease on life when I started my network marketing business.

For the thirteen years before starting my network marketing business, I worked full time for the Australian federal government. I also ran a business with my husband, and we had our wonderful little girl, Izabella. My life was full. But there were two large problems with this schedule of working seventy-plus hours a week. The first, and most significant, was that I often couldn't be there with

Izabella when it mattered. The hardest moments came when I took her to school and couldn't stay for assemblies like the other mums. It broke my heart to see her disappointed little face. I knew I had to find another way, so I could be there for Izabella always. The second problem was flexibility. Being in the traditional nine-to-five environment didn't give me the chance for life-changing income and flexibility, two of the things everyone wants. I craved more freedom and control.

Then, in one day, or actually in one phone call, my whole life changed forever. I was offered a network marketing business. At first I was sceptical, but I knew that if I didn't make a different choice right then, nothing would change. It was up to me to determine my destiny.

Within seven months, I was a vice president, with my company replacing my fulltime income. I continued to keep at my hectic schedule, until I resigned from my government job just twelve months after starting my network marketing business. I began attending Izabella's assemblies, and I was even able to help out in the classroom. Also, in one of my happiest moments, my husband was finally able to resign from a job he was not happy with but held for twenty years to support us. Now he gets to enjoy a job he really wants. It's completely transformed his life.

After being in the industry and running my business for just over three years, I have just hit the top of our management structure and looking at an average income of $25,000 a month. The top economists are predicting a growth of six-hundred precent in network marketing. It's not a matter of *if* but *when*.

This will become the next trillion-dollar industry, with the next wave of millionaires predicted to come out of network marketing companies, specifically in health and wellness. It's the scariest decision I've ever made, but I'm so grateful to have jumped into it, because I'm creating a legacy for my family and my daughter's family that will impact them for generations to come. In most network marketing companies your business is willable, so I can pass this income on to my family forever.

I now have a massive passion to show people, especially women, how they, too, can have it all and not rely on others for financial freedom. I get the honour to help, coach, and train, but my passion is to show women a different choice and allow them to put their passion first and foremost, so they have the chance to

CHAPTER 14: Rebecca McIntyre

make life-changing money at the same time. This is the industry that will make will make it come true, with six out of ten women who earn over $100,000 a year coming from the network marketing industry.

There is a choice, and I'm so thankful I chose network marketing. I now look forward to helping others for the rest of my life. I love what I do, so it doesn't feel like work. I get to take time off when I want and travel the world, because my business is run on-line, and that can happen from anywhere in the world there's Internet. On-line businesses are the way of the future.

I continue to live in my small country town and give my daughter the country upbringing my husband and I always envisioned for her, close to her grandparents and family. But I also have the means to take her travelling all over the world to see and experience different cultures and educate her in any school I want, so together we can run organisations and programs to give back to my community. This is all possible, because I stepped out of my comfort zone and believed in myself and what was possible. I also believed I deserved more, and so did my family. Now, three years later, I run a multi-million dollar business earning life-changing money, all from my home in a small county town. I've barely started, but the future is so bright, and my dreams are so big. How does it get any better than that?

Think about it. You can create a residual income that's not dependant on you, so if you're no longer around, your business keeps running. That's the secret of network marketing. Creating a duplicate business not dependant on you, because you don't trade time for money. You can do it all and get paid amazingly well. You have so many choices. You just have to know where to look.

"Passion fuels the rocket, but vision — a big dream —points the rocket to its ultimate destination. DREAM BIG."

Steve Jobs

CHAPTER 15

Yeukai Ota

CHAPTER FIFTEEN

Yeukai Ota

Tell me about your early life

I was born to high-achieving parents. My late father was a doctor in philosophy, and my mother was a chief computer programmer. My early years were spent in the United States of America in Washington, D.C. My mother has strong family roots, so in 1991 my family relocated back to Zimbabwe after living in the U.S. for eight years.

My mother wanted us to learn our cultural heritage. Being a strict disciplinarian, she wanted to raise us to be bold, resilient women and men who knew their roots. Growing up in suburban Harare, we were always confined to the corners of our house. We lived on an acre block that had a large security wall and gate that was always locked. My sisters and brother were my best friends.

As I grew older I was allowed only a few other friends who pretty much lived a life that mirrored mine. A lot of my time was spent reading books or playing imaginary games with my Barbie dolls. I attended a Catholic girls-only high school. We were brought up on the philosophy of being equal and at oneness with everybody. From a young age I distinguished myself from the other children. It would be more precise to say I was different. I was extremely passionate about helping people and making a difference in their lives. I always wound up in the position of nurturing and advocating in one way or the other, no matter who it was. My mission was to make a difference. This sometimes meant getting into trouble, but that didn't stop me. I was determined. I wanted to make a notable difference in people's lives. This became a part of my genetic makeup.

My life took a notable twist in 1999, when I was only fourteen. I lost my father after his long battle with Bowel Cancer. I was devastated. My perfect world had come caving in, but I was determined to find the cause of this disease to ensure no one else would be robbed by it.

CHAPTER 15: Yeukai Ota

What did you do?

Destiny led me to Nursing.

At nineteen years of age, I embarked on this amazing Journey. I travelled to Australia from Harare Zimbabwe, otherwise known as the Sunshine City, to pursue a Bachelor of Science in Nursing. My father had prepared well for our future by taking out long-term investments and a healthy life insurance policy. His dream was for us to attend university in any part of the world we decided on. His dream had come true.

As I was leaving home, I only took four items with me. The first was my passport, which suddenly became my most valuable possession. Second, the last piece of advice my mother gave me, which was "You better hold tight onto this document. This is what will be used to identify you but never let it define you. We are not defined by where we are from but by how much of our self-limiting beliefs we are willing to give up. Set goals and dream." Third, thirty kg of baggage, which was all I could carry. I quickly learnt to let go in order to receive more. And lastly, I had a dream.

I got onto a thirteen-hour Qantas Flight to Perth. This is when I began my early adult life and what I consider the real school of life.

It was by far the hardest thing I'd ever done and by far my greatest achievement. In this process I realised I had more power inside of me than I thought. The power I'm talking about is the force that propelled me. I developed a coping strategy I call my mantras or rituals.

What are your mantras?

1. **Have gratitude.**

Beginning the day with gratitude sets the altitude and latitude for the day.

My first apartment was in Mosman Park in Perth. I looked for any area that was close to the university, had reliable transportation, entertainment, employment, affordable rentals, and was close to the beach. My mother had sent me off with enough money for six months' rent. After that I had to find my own way. I set my intentions to look for a place that did not compromise on my comfort but still within my budget. I wanted to get off to a good start and in an environment that was conducive. If you want to be more productive, try turning your space into your personal haven. I chose a one-bedroom student pad with scenic views. It was the perfect spot for me.

Every day I would wake up early, open the blinds to my bedroom, and look out into the expanse as I dreamed. I began my day with gratitude for this amazing view. It did not matter what else was going on. I thought about nothing else for those twenty minutes of my day. I began a gratitude journal, as I wanted to relive these moments daily. All of a sudden, my gratitude grew and extended even to the not-so-nice things that were happening in my life. Everything became a learning experience rather than a setback, and so I became grateful for the learning experience. People would ask me why I was always so happy. They wanted to know what my secret was.

My mindset had changed, and it had an effect on all other areas of my life. I began to excel in my studies from an average student to top of the class. I became confident and started to attract good things. I was proud to be a woman and embraced my femininity.

My advice to stay in happiness and gratitude is to change your mind set. Defeat and failure become a choice. When you change your mindset, it's like resetting yourself or adjusting yourself. You think a lot better and see things more clearly. We all have a conqueror and a victim within us. It's a choice which one we let shine. You can practice by beginning with being grateful for little things and then increasing your gratitude.

2. **Speak less and listen more.**

My English was very good, and I was an articulate speaker. I had always excelled at language and arts in school. In Australia, my biggest challenge was the dialect. When I spoke, people would ask where I was from. In turn, the Australian accent was difficult for me to understand, as people spoke faster. I needed to adapt and learn to speak again.

You learn a lot more from listening rather than speaking. Listening is like a sixth sense. Most people don't really listen. They are quick to speak. Listening gives you time to process what you are about to say. Planned silence, as I like to call it, gives you leverage to provide an intelligent response and not answer

CHAPTER 15: Yeukai Ota

from an emotional place. Often when we learn the art of listening and allow this to become a part of who you are, it becomes a game changer. Everything that's being invented in the universe is a replication of something that has already been created. Learning from those who have already experienced that life lesson helps you to build your knowledge. Listening helps you to tap into the little whispers of life. You could go further if you begin to learn the act of listening.

3. Go the extra mile.

Successful people plan their steps.

Everything I wanted to achieve I had achieved. I tried out a lot of different things as a student. I set goals for myself, both short and long term. Being an international student, I had to work that much harder and put in more hours and effort to become a master at what I was learning .To do that, I had to be strategic. I had to be purposeful.

To be master at something is to be the go-to person for that product or service. According to Maslow's hierarchy of needs, self-actualisation is the highest of all human needs. Therefore, billions of people are looking for leaders in their field to help them get to self-actualisation. In order to be a leader, you need to be purposeful and intentional. This can be broken down to the way you present yourself, your image, the knowledge you have, the people you surround yourself with, and how you spend your time. Study successful people in the area in which you want to develop mastery. Seek wisdom and understanding through acquiring knowledge. Be creative. Make it a point to learn something new every single day.

The force that propels me and gets me out of bed each morning is my desire to help people and see lives transformed. My family is the fire that keeps me alight and so passionate. They are my *Why*. What keeps me challenged and going is my faith.

I have fallen in love with the things that seemed to be my greatest setbacks, for they have helped me get leverage for my most successful comebacks. The more I embraced challenges, the less focussed on them, and the more I conquered my fears. This helped me go that extra mile.

Life is like a training ground. It is a school that equips us with the essential tools and life skills we need to get to our destiny. The one thing we are created for.

I am now qualified as a Registered Nurse. The highlight of my career is being selected the International Association of Nurses board as a mentor for nurses and upcoming nurses across the globe. My career has given me the privilege to touch so many lives. Countless, to be precise. Working alongside one of the top general surgeons, I now have an in-depth knowledge about bowel cancer, the disease that robbed me of my father. I have built my empire around helping people make better life and health choices. This is just a snippet of what is to come. My dream is to make a notable difference beyond my wildest imagination.

I have reinvented myself, and at the age of thirty one, my title is wife to my amazing husband. I also have the title of Mother to my miracle son, born after twenty-seven weeks of gestation and fought for his life against all odds. Being a Peri-operative Registered Nurse is my passion. Being Chief Executive Officer and Founder to Micah Group of companies is one of my purposes. My purposes are diversified, from life coaching and health, beauty, and wellness, to advertising and marketing, as well as mining and construction. I will continue to reinvent myself as I follow my dream and live to my maximum potential. That's what I have been created for.

My life is a testimony that there are no barriers to success except for the ones we put up for ourselves or allow to define how far we can go. Every day is a new dawn with endless possibilities and an opportunity to reinvent yourself.

DREAM BIG.

Conclusion

After spending hours interviewing these wonderful women, I was left with a sense of awe and a belief that this world is full of great people who have faced challenges and still find the courage to rise above it to do great work. I hope you've received this book's central message: love yourself and be a catalyst for change.

Just by altering your perception and believing in yourself like these women did, you can, and will, make a positive difference to those around you.

> *"I have learned over the years that when one's mind is made up, this diminishes fear; knowing what must be done does away with fear."*
>
> Rosa Parks

Resources

For more information, please visit:

www.nkandubeltz.com.au

www.fierceandfabulous.com.au

www.motivationalspeakersaustralia.com/nkandubeltz

You can also buy merchandise from our online store such as jewellery, diaries, notebooks, and other titles by Nkandu Beltz.

About The Author
Nkandu Beltz

Nkandu Beltz discovered from an early age that little acts of kindness have the power to make a positive and lasting change in the world. For over two decades, this passionate human rights activist has been a voice for the voiceless and has found the courage to stand up for those who could not stand up for themselves. And yet, she still has so much to give.

Growing up in Zambia, Nkandu was acutely aware of the social disparity she, and many others, faced. The injustice was overwhelming for the free-spirited young girl and not something she could easily ignore. Encouraged by her father to stand up for what she believed in, Nkandu began petitioning for girl child rights at the age of ten.

Making change in the world is in everything she does. Whether she's mentoring young people, developing a new community program, or raising awareness for important issues like HIV/AIDS and domestic violence, Nkandu is devoted to helping others live a better life. She's a member of UN women and a HeForShe leader. Nkandu is passionate about empowering women.

Her incredible journey has led her across the globe to Australia, where she now lives with her husband and three children in country Victoria. It's here, supported by her family, that she continues her mission.

After sharing her personal experience facing up to social injustice in her book *I Have the Power*, she brings us *Fierce & Fabulous* that delves into the lives of extraordinary women who've overcome tremendous challenges to achieve their dreams.

Other books by Nkandu Beltz:

I Have the Power

Welcome to the tear-jerking and uplifting life story of a social change-maker and humanitarian: Nkandu Beltz. In her first published book, *I Have The Power,* Nkandu shares her entire story from being born as a 'girl child' in Zambia through to her life here in Australia today.

By recounting her adversities, including being poisoned, as well as the many extraordinary experiences she has been blessed to have in life like interviewing the Dalai Lama, Nkandu aims to inspire every reader to realize that they DO have the power to change the world.

A book that stays with you long after you read it, *I Have the Power* is set to inspire people around the world to find *their* own amazing journey and make a difference to the lives of others.

Emily Gowor
Author, Publisher, and Speaker

About The Author

Fierce and Fabulous Diaries

Have you ever wondered how some people seem to succeed at everything they do? We want to help you find their mission and clear your vision to live an inspired life. We are dedicated to helping you live the best life you can.

The women featured in this book are highly skilled at what they do.

You can sign up for workshops around the country on varies topics, as well as hear more about these fierce and fabulous women through webinars and podcasts.

As the architect of Fierce & Fabulous, I hope you will join me on this inspirational journey by becoming a part of our community and creating an environment for the next generation to flourish and thrive.

You might want to purchase one of our inspirational, limited-edition Fierce and Fabulous diaries.

For more details, send an email to admin@nkandubeltz.com.au or visit us at www.fierceandfabulous.com.au.

Want to be a Published Author?

Writing and publishing your very own book does not have to be hard. You just need to have a message to share.

At Author Express we love to turn your publishing dreams into a reality. If you are;

- **A Difference-Maker** - People that have a message they want to share to make a difference in the world
- **A Business Owner** -The best business card on the planet is a book
- **A Writer** – You've written your book and just want to know the most effective way to publish it, then we would love to help.

To find out how you can **Share Your Message, Make a Difference and Leave a Legacy** ™ simply go to www.AuthorExpress.com

www.ingramcontent.com/pod-product-compliance
Lightning Source LLC
Chambersburg PA
CBHW050533300426
44113CB00012B/2069